More Memories

of
Chester

Part of the
Memories
series

More Memories

of

Chester

Edited by Elaine Pierce Jones

*The Publishers would like to thank the following companies for supporting
the production of this book*

Main Sponsor

Weinholts of Chester

The Biggins Sargent Partnership

Bookland of Chester

British United Turkeys Limited

Chester Markets

Cochranes of Chester

Henry R Davis & Company

Dutton & Hallmark

Lowes of Chester

Montgomery Tomlinson

First published in Great Britain by True North Books Limited
Units 3 - 5 Heathfield Industrial Park
Elland West Yorkshire
HX5 9AE
Tel. 01422 377977
© Copyright: True North Books Limited 2000

ISBN 1 903204 02 X

Text, design and origination by True North Books Limited
Printed and bound by The Amadeus Press Limited

Memories are made of this

Memories. We all have them: people, places and events, some good and some bad. Our memories of the place where we grew up are usually tucked away in a very special place in our mind. The best are probably connected with our childhood and youth, when we longed to be grown up and paid no attention to adults who told us to enjoy being young, as these were the best years of our lives. We look back now and realise that they were right.

Old photographs bring our memories flooding back - coronations and celebrations; talking pictures, Technicolor and television; the war years, rationing, and the shared hopes and fears which created such a warm community spirit; buying things made of nylon and plastic; fashions which took trouserbottoms and hemlines from drainpipes and mini-skirts to the other extreme; Doris Day, Acker Bilk, Elvis Presley and the Beatles; the jitterbug, the tango and discos; Ford Populars and Minis; decimalisation. Life changed so much over the years. Some changes were big, some small; some altered our lives in ways we never anticipated. Who in the early days of motoring could have foreseen the motorways and traffic systems of the latter decades of the 20th century? Did any of us realise, when we first saw a computer, what a tremendous impact they would have on our lives?

Self-service supermarkets and frozen food made our lives easier - but at the expense of our friendly little corner shops. Nostalgia is always such a mixture of feelings . . . We hope that the collection of pictures in this book will remind you of happy days in bygone eras - and who knows, you might even have been there when one of the photographs was taken!

Contents

Around the city centre

Chester Library

I f the fashions of the day are anything to go by, the day in question captured by this photograph must have been around 1930. The ladies' hats have a definite pre-war feel about them, as does the sturdy bone-shaker pram. Things were made to last in those days! The buildings on view, however, present much the same image to the photographer today as they did around 70 years ago. This applies particularly to the magnificent structure on the corner of Eastgate Street and Bridge Street, built by Thomas Lockwood for the Duke of Westminster in 1888. Not only this, but Walton the jewellers still trade there, as

they did around 1930. Generally speaking, however, businesses come and go, and Hudson Verity no longer provide spectacles at 5 Bridge Street. This junction at the heart of Chester is marked by the High Cross, a site of such history and tradition that the Town Crier still puts in an appearance there during the summer months. The city government of Mayor, Aldermen and Councilmen met at the Cross for almost 300 years from 1506, using a timber-framed building known as the Pentice. On a darker note, these centuries also saw the area of the Cross being used for the barbarous 'sport' of bull-baiting with dogs.

Chester Library

Both pictures: Thirty years or more separate these two photographs taken at roughly the same spot, the junction of Eastgate Street and St Werburgh Street, looking towards the Cathedral. The pictures give a good impression of that mixture of change and continuity which characterised so much of the city centre's streets between the 1930s and the 1960s. Continuity is best expressed not only by the dominating presence of the Cathedral, but also by the architecture along St Werburgh Street. This remained pretty much unchanged between these decades, and indeed this still applies today. The best angle for an appreciation of this is provided by the 1964 shot *(above)*. The handsome buildings on the right were designed and developed by John Douglas, in imitation Renaissance style, between 1895 and 1899. The half timbered-effect was a result of the Duke of Westminster's insistence, and the width of the street was doubled by this development. Originally it had been no more than a narrow lane leading to the Cathedral. Other Chester triumphs for Douglas included buildings along Grosvenor Park Road and the Diamond Jubilee Clock at Eastgate. As a contrast the entrance to the left, by the No Entry sign, gives a hint of the fine

classical style building which is now occupied by the National Westminster Bank.

For change, of course, one need look no further than the inexorable rise of the motor-car. The 1930s scene on the left shows a fairly quiet two-way street, with a small amount of traffic visible towards the far end. It must have been a 'busy' part of the day, for a white-coated policeman is on traffic duty, but it looks as if he has plenty of time to give a good, long look at the camera. In contrast, the policeman in the 1964 shot is in much busier mode, and the pedestrians pour across the junction as soon as they get the chance. A one-way system is in operation - in itself an indicator of a rising volume of traffic. The car age really did begin in the 1960s as rising prosperity allowed many more people to afford this luxury, often through 'hire-purchase' agreements. A brand new Morris 1000 retailed at around £515 in 1964, whilst a Hillman Imp cost £532. If these prices sound incredibly cheap, it has to be remembered that such amounts might represent close to a year's wages for many ordinary working people. Would your annual income be swallowed up by the cost of a basic saloon car today?

The architecture which graces this corner was built for the Duke of Westminster in 1888

This may well be one of Chester's most photogenic spots, and rightly so. The High Cross which marks the junction of the city's four main streets - Eastgate, Bridge, Watergate and Northgate - is rich in both history and visual appeal. This particular photograph was taken around 1930, and as with any shot from this era an array of headgear is on view. Cloche hats are strongly represented amongst the ladies, but the gentlemen on or around the famous steps sport a bowler, a trilby, a homburg and a humble flat cap. The wonderful architecture which graces this corner was the work of Thomas Lockwood, built in Renaissance style for the Duke of Westminster in 1888. The High Cross itself was erected in 1407, providing a meeting place and a bargaining spot for merchants until the Civil War of the 1640s. Then it was broken up, and after its reconstruction at Netherleigh House it stayed in the grounds there for some time before being erected in the Roman Gardens adjoining Newgate. Finally the High Cross returned to its rightful place in 1975. It is not exactly a serene spot today, for it teems with shoppers and visitors, but in past times it served as a convenient venue for settling differences, as with the master weavers and the journeymen, who fought it out at the Cross in 1399!

CARS, CHAOS AND COST

Britain saw its very first car in 1894. Twenty years later, in 1914, the world's first traffic lights were installed in front of the House of Commons. Cars were here to stay - but they brought with them their own particular problems.

As traffic levels increased in town centres around the country, various schemes were put in place to control the flow. Some involved the motorist's pocket; in 1947 a Road Tax of £1 per year was imposed.

Road safety also became a major issue, and in 1956 the Ministry of Transport introduced road testing, which at first only affected cars more than ten years old.

To the frustration of the many motorists who were used to free parking, parking meters were introduced to Britain in June, 1958. At the same time, yellow no-waiting lines came into force. A whole new way of life began for the British driver.

It would be intriguing to know the subject of the conversation between the car driver and the policeman on Eastgate Street at some point in the early 1950s. It looks as if the policeman is just donning his white gloves to go on point duty. Traffic lights, filters and direction lanes have largely replaced this part of police work. No doubt this has helped to relieve pressure on stretched police manpower, but the presence of a policeman on point duty certainly instilled a good deal of discipline into

Chester Library

drivers. No 'jumping the lights' or taking unexpected turns with them around! On the contrary, not only did you sit quietly and await the signal to go, you always had that uneasy feeling that the policeman might stroll across and start asking questions about your tax returns or your TV licence. Perhaps in this photograph the policeman is casting some doubts on the roadwor-

thiness of this Morris 10/4 saloon, which was an 'old-timer' even in the 1950s. The chief point of interest amongst the shop frontages is the sign for Browns of Chester in the top left-hand corner. This renowned local enterprise was founded by Susannah Brown in the late eighteenth century, and still exists today, with its 'Five Floors of Fashion and Furnishing'.

Chester Archives: ref CH 1140

It seems remarkably quiet on Bridge Street, looking towards the junction with Watergate Street, considering that this formed part of the main highway through Chester towards Wales, via the Grosvenor Bridge. The fact that this was 1944, however, goes some way towards an explanation. Economy in support of the war effort was the keynote of the time. Non-essential car travel was frowned upon - 'Is your journey really necessary?' - and petrol rationing enforced the message. Cycling was one way to overcome such difficulties, unless of course the bicycle 'played up', which is possibly the situation in the foreground, to the right. Perhaps the renowned John Bull Puncture Repair Outfit was about to go into action. Willerbys (tailors), the English Leather Company and Siddalls (opticians) are just some of the retail businesses on view. If Bridge Street presents a rather 'grey' appearance, this is not entirely due to the age of the photograph. Twenty years later a brightening up programme began the process which has made the street look so attractive today. Shopping with ration books must also have been a 'grey' business, and the ladies crossing the street may well have been seeking something to brighten up some of the suggested government recipes, such as carrot marmalade!

Below centre: There seems to be a chill in the air judging by the way the two United States servicemen are wrapped up, and the same applies to the two women and the child further on. This rather fine shot along the top of the Eastgate towards the famous old clock was taken in 1944, and no doubt that the two servicemen were seeing the sights of Chester. The view down Foregate Street that they were enjoying is a good one, and they could not have failed to appreciate the fine Flemish style building in the background, then the Midland Bank, to the left. This master-piece of Victorian Gothic in red brick and stone was built by John Douglas, in 1883-4. The sightseers were close enough to get a very good view of the Eastgate Clock, with its beautiful and intricate ironwork designed by James Swindley, a blacksmith from Handbridge. Tourists love stunning statistics, and perhaps the fact that the pendulum weighs over one hundredweight (50 kg) might have impressed the US visitors. A statistic that lay over half a century on from 1944 , but an interesting one nevertheless, is that prints of the Eastgate Clock bought by visitors consume over one tonne of paper each year!

Chester Archives: ref CH 1142

Bottom: E Dutton & Sons, Undertakers, along with the City Arms public house, are the most prominent commercial premises in view in this shot of Frodsham Street in 1944. A funeral parlour has little need of an attractive exterior to generate custom, but it is always useful for a pub to have some aesthetic appeal. The early nineteenth century City Arms filled the bill nicely in this respect, and not only on the outside, for it was also well-known for the beautiful crest above its fireplace. Street names often contain a good deal of history, but the title of Frodsham Street seems pretty straightforward - the route linking Frodsham with Chester. However, until the nineteenth century it was known as Cow Lane, which conjures up more interesting possibilities, of cattle markets or slaughterhouses. The photograph suggests a nip in the air, judging by the warm clothing being worn. People seem to be moving briskly, none more so than the serviceman approaching on the bicycle. Military personnel visiting Chester from nearby camps were a common sight in 1944. Even the famous Roodeye racecourse housed an ordnance store and ATS girls were stationed there. Some of the latter were no doubt regulars at the War Services Women's Club on Watergate Street, or at the canteen on nearby Queen Street.

Chester Archives: ref CH 1151

Chester Library

Left: In Roman times the Eastgate marked the eastern exit of the fortress, and technically speaking military rule ended here. Foregate Street developed as a civilian community set up 'before the gate'. Trade must have figured strongly as a reason for doing this, and this picture of Foregate Street in 1944, looking from the Eastgate down to the junction with Frodsham Street, shows trade strongly represented in the shape of Stead & Simpson (shoes), WH Smith (books) and J Brassey & Son (ironmongery and cycles). The 'household' name of WH Smith continues today. The area between Frodsham Street and the next junction, Queen Street, was mentioned in the city records as the Jousting Croft in 1472, which conjures up a colourful image of horses, lances and flying pennants. It may have been this historical aspect of Chester which captured the imagination of the photographer, Robert Astrella. He was a member of the United States Air Force, and although stationed near Oxford, he took a series of photographs of Chester in 1944. Some servicemen appear on this one, and they would have been a familiar wartime sight, for there were training camps at the Dale, Upton and at Saighton. Fighter pilots were trained at the RAF station at Hawarden and at its satellite airfield at Poulton.

Above: As befits a postcard, some of the most notable features of this section of Eastgate are given prominence in a scene that has a 1940s air about it. The main focus of the shot is the Grosvenor Hotel, which dominates the right-hand side of the street above the Huxley's sign. The Grosvenor name is liberally dotted about Chester, for as well as the hotel it can be found as a prefix to a park, a bridge, a street, a road, a museum and a shopping precinct. The Grosvenor family had very close links with Chester, and when the Dukedom of Westminster was created in 1874, the first Duke of Westminster was Hugh Lupus Grosvenor. He and his successors sponsored many buildings in Chester. The Grosvenor Hotel was designed and built in grand style by TM Penson between 1863 and 1866, although it had to be completed by others after his death. Other well-known buildings on Eastgate that Penson left his mark on were the Browns Crypt Buildings and the 'black and white' section of the Browns of Chester store. The arch of the old Eastgate itself is clearly visible in the background, representing a tradition of gates at this point which dates back to Roman times.

The imitation Renaissance style of architecture, or 'black and white', is very well illustrated in this photograph of the Rows at the Cross. These buildings are certainly beautiful and stylish, and instantly transport visitors back some three or four hundred years in time. It comes of something of a shock,

then, to learn that many of them are Victorian creations, very late Victorian in the case of the two featured here. The wonderful structure dominating the foreground was built by Thomas Lockwood for the Duke of Westminster in 1888, and the same architect was responsible for the building towards the right, across Bridge Street, in 1892.

Nevertheless these structures do form a genuine part of Chester's long and rich history, a heritage of which Cestrians are justly proud. For example, close to the sign for Bridge Street is another one, 'Via Pretoria', a reminder of those days when Chester was a Roman fortress situated on a sandstone spur in a loop of the River Dee - a perfect defensive base. The headquarters of Deva, as the Romans called it, would have stood here, at the intersection or 'cross' of the four principal streets. The serviceman and his lady friend, taking a stroll on Eastgate Street in this 1940s photograph, have history all around them, even beneath their feet.

Chester Library

Above: If Chester has plenty of imitation Renaissance buildings, then this is the genuine article. Ye Olde King's Head, at the corner of Lower Bridge Street and Castle Street, was built in 1621, and the timber-framed structure was enhanced by unusual herringbone design across the top storey. It was built on the site of an even earlier structure, the first stone building in Chester, and it is known that Peter the Clerk lived here in 1208. He was the chief officer of Earl Ranulph III, being a forerunner of later mayors, and he was allowed to hold his own court and keep a fishing boat on the River Dee. In the seventeenth and early eighteenth centuries, Ye Olde King's Head was home to successive Randle Holmes of Cheshire, four of whom were antiquarians and herald painters. This photograph was taken in 1948, when the inn was retailing Wilderspool Ales. The shop to the right gives an indication that selling antiques is nothing new to Chester. The property to the left, at the far side of Castle Street, looks a little dilapidated, but there is no doubt that bus 'buffs' will love the sight of the fine old vehicle emerging at the bottom of the street.

The original Eastgate is said to have had Roman arches built into it

Right: Congestion galore is the image presented by this 1951 photograph of the Eastgate. Traffic is squeezing its way in both directions through the arch and pedestrians throng the pavements. The policeman on point duty certainly has his work cut out! It would not have been much consolation to those caught up in this frantic rush to know that congestion had been taking place at the Eastgate for centuries past. Eastgate Street was one of the main streets (the Via Principalis in fact) of Roman Chester, and from that time until the twentieth century horses, wagons and carts played their part in clogging up the Eastgate. Relatively recent times have seen pedestrianisation and a safer environment for shoppers and sightseers. The present Eastgate was built in 1768-9 at the expense of Richard, Lord Grosvenor. The old Medieval gate is said to have had Roman arches built into it. One of the finest buildings on the street can be seen adjoining the Eastgate. Built of stone and red brick in 1883 by John Douglas, and enlarged in 1908, its turrets give it a Dutch or Flemish appearance. Now housing the HSBC Bank, the building carries the 12 shields of the old counties of Wales, and the Owen Jones memorial to a local butcher who was a great benefactor to the poor.

F. W. WOOLWORTH & C[?]

BALDOMAH

KINGS ARMS
KITCHEN

EKF 56

The Browns building, built in 1856 was the first of Chester's famous 'black and white' structures

Eastgate has been caught from a high elevation in August 1966, and if ever two cars symbolised that dynamic decade from the motoring point of view, they were the Mini and the Morris Minor. One of each can be seen, and many people buying a car for the first time found their dreams realised in the distinctive lines of these models. The age of mass car ownership had really begun! Distinction of a different kind belongs to three buildings all associated with Browns, but with greatly differing styles. At far right is the Browns Crypt Building, built in High Victorian Gothic style by Penson in 1858. Next comes a touch of the Classical as the bus queue stretches past columns that were erected in 1828. The final Browns building, next to the bus and designed by Penson in 1856, was the first of Chester's Victorian 'black and white' structures. The Eastgate arch, in the background, is associated with yet another famous Chester name. It was built in 1768-9 at the expense of Richard, Lord Grosvenor, replacing a Medieval gateway. The ornamental Eastgate clock, visible above the arch, was supposed to have celebrated Queen Victoria's Diamond Jubilee in 1897. In fact, because it was not in position until May 1899, it turned out to be a celebration of the Queen's 80th birthday!

A Morris Minor and a Standard 10, plus the style of the wagon, the bus and the British Road Services van, place this view up Bridge Street fairly firmly in the 1950s. The street name of White Friars, to the far left, has an interesting derivation, being named after white-robed Carmelite Friars, who founded a local monastery in 1277. To the right , just behind the tail of the wagon, Feathers Lane once led to the Feathers Hotel, Chester's prime nineteenth century coaching inn, which was demolished in 1866. Further up Bridge Street, again to the right, is the imposing and unmistakable entrance to St Michael's

Chester Library

Arcade, rebuilt in 'Chester black and white' in 1912 after citizens protested at the original (1910) white tile facade. Some of the Bridge Street names that were very familiar to 1950s shoppers have now gone, including Creamers Furriers and the Imperial Typewriter Depot, both on the right. The latter was part of the Typewriter Exchange Company, and the Depot remained at these Bridge Street premises until 1975. St Peter's Church provides a nice focal point in the background. The Church is unusual in not having a nave and being almost square in shape. The spire on the tower was to be later removed.

Left: The buildings along Eastgate Street look in fine fettle in this photograph of July 29th 1966, and so they should have done, for this date marked the official opening of the newly redecorated and refurbished street. Two years earlier the traders of Bridge Street had carried out an improvement scheme to highlight its attractions, and the Eastgate traders followed suit in 1966. The well-known shop names of the day are prominent, including Henry Fields, Collinson & Co, and Walton the jewellers. Traffic was halted or diverted for some time to allow the opening ceremony to take place, and the driver of the Morris Traveller estate car was probably unaware of how well his 'half-timbered car' fitted in with the half-timbered structures all around! Lord Kennett, a prominent government figure, ceremonially cut a ribbon and went on walkabout with leading figures in the scheme. There must have been a little friendly rivalry in the air, for the chairman of the Eastgate Street Traders' Committee, Mr IC Halliwell, received a congratulatory telegram from his Bridge Street counterpart, Mr J Welsby, but one which also pointed out that Bridge Street had led the way - 'We lead, others follow.' Mr Halliwell, in his reply, let it be known that Eastgate Street was still 'Via Principalis' - Main Street!

Below: Eastgate Street, from the area of the Gate itself as far as the Cross, is not an unusual view for visitors to admire. In terms of the architecture it could be a modern shot, particularly the view of the fine buildings on opposite corners of St Werburgh Street - the handsome Classical lines of what is now the National Westminster Bank offsetting the 'black and white' style of the building currently occupied by Barclays. However, the photograph was taken in more sombre times, 1944 to be precise, when the preoccupations of war were probably uppermost in the minds of those who were passing along Eastgate Street. St Peter's Church, visible in the background and still with its spire at this date, has an unusual connection with war and peace. In the days of the two annual Medieval fairs in the city, a wooden hand was displayed in the area of the Cross for 14 days before each fair. This was to symbolise the King's peace for the duration of the fair - an amnesty to known criminals. This hand hung from St Peter's from 1803, until the custom was dropped and it was sold for 'two pints of ale'. Eventually the symbol of peace ended up in Liverpool Museum - where German bombs destroyed it in World War II!

Chester Archives: ref CH 1873

A gloomy looking and damp day in 1951 nevertheless sees a busy Eastgate as the camera takes in a long shot as far as the Cross, where a bus is just turning out of Bridge Street. Free use is being made of the street by an assortment of 'period' vehicles, and the front car in the line parked on the left must have been one of the earliest of the Morris Minor models. The old fashioned open-back bus is a reminder of those days when a quick sprint and a daring leap might well 'save your bacon' if you had just missed the bus even though the conductor often took a dim view of it. A very well-known commercial name in Chester is visible at bottom right in the shape of B Walton, specialising in watches and silver. This firm also had premises in the fine building on the corner of Eastgate Street and Bridge Street, and still does. Further up Eastgate, on the left, are the three completely different frontages which, together, make up the one store of Browns of Chester. Crowds of shoppers throng the pavements, but choice would still have been limited, for the rationing of the war years did not totally disappear until 1954.

WATCHES
B. WALTON & SO
SILVERWARE

A similar scene looking up Eastgate Street, albeit from a slightly different angle, shows a world that had changed in many ways by the time of the 1960s. 'Swinging' this decade might have been, but it was also an age of increasing restrictions as the rising tide of traffic threatened to engulf city centres. The onset of the dreaded yellow line seems to be having the desired effect with regard to parking on the street, although a few car owners appear to be flouting the rules. Pedestrians are having a much easier time of it than on the 1951 shot; the age of pedestrianisation was on its way. Another change

was the amount of money that shoppers had in their pockets by the 1960s, and the range of goods available. Of course some things were much the same, for example the shops and stores to the right - Waltons, Woolworth and Kardomah. On the opposite side of the street the Grosvenor Hotel sign still sported the family's early arms - a golden wheatsheaf on a blue background. Continuity is perhaps best expressed in the architecture. Plenty of 'black and white' structures can be seen, but the classical columns of the National Westminster Bank, on the corner of St Werburgh Street, look truly outstanding.

Chester Library

Chester Library

Chester Library

Above: 'Old and ugly', was Daniel Defoe's description of Chester's unique Rows in the early eighteenth century. The historian Camden, on the other hand, marvelled at shopping galleries 'through which a man may walk dry from one end to the other'. Most visitors find themselves on the side of Camden, and if there is one memory of Chester that remains in their minds it is that of those wonderfully distinctive wooden arcades. This remarkable wide-angle shot shows the Rows on Eastgate Street and Bridge Street to good effect. The vehicles on view date the photograph to the 1930s, perhaps earlier, but the presence of a white-coated policeman on point duty along Eastgate Street reveals that there was a traffic problem even then. It is likely that the first Rows were built in Chester in 1278 after a terrible fire had caused great destruction. Many Rows were lost between 1600 and 1650, particularly in Northgate Street, Foregate Street and Lower Bridge Street. The current appearance of the Rows, reflected in the photograph, is a product of nineteenth century enterprise and vision. From around 1850 Victorian architects led the 'black and white revival', which managed to create stylish building of seemingly great antiquity.

Above right: A couple of scraps of litter mar what is an otherwise interesting view of Eastgate Street at gallery level from Bridge Street. So little have the essential features of this view changed that the photograph could have been taken at almost any moment in this century. What a first glance might miss, however, is the sight of a motor-car, partly obscured by the rails. This grand but rather antique vehicle immediately puts a 1920s stamp on the scene. The Etonian, a well-established tailoring and gents' outfitting concern on the corner of Eastgate Street

and Northgate Street, is no longer with us. The firm of H Samuel currently occupies that corner, and the buildings stretching away into the background display that fascinating blend of brick and 'black and white' which is so distinctive to Chester. Equally distinctive are the wooden arcades, or Rows, one of which frames this shot. Although direct descendants of the Medieval Rows, the modern versions bear little resemblance to their ancestors. It needs a leap of the imagination to envisage the complex network of steps, ladders and narrow walkways which linked shops and houses. Goods for sale would be crammed into every space and hung from the rafters, creating a rich medley of sights and aromas.

Below: Planning and redevelopment became the name of the game in 1960s and 70s Britain. Rising prosperity meant that money was available to sweep away some of the more unsightly legacies of the past and propel Britain into the modern age. This planning model for the redevelopment of the area contained by Princess Street and Linenhall Street, behind the Town Hall, was first put on public display in September 1960. The scheme involved the demolition of much poor quality terraced housing, and its replacement by a new market, municipal offices, shops and a new coach station. There was to be car-parking for 800 vehicles, and a pedestrian way linking Market Square with the new market and Princess Street. As we have since learned to our cost, redevelopment schemes of this era had a habit of bulldozing everything in their path, fine and historic buildings as well as slums. With its rich architectural heritage, Chester was in a very vulnerable position in this respect, and from the outset the local Civic Trust was insisting on safeguards. Work proceeded from the mid 1960s into the early 1970s, the old Market Hall being demolished in 1967. More redesigning came in 1994-5, and such features as The Forum and the Gateway Theatre are now an integral part of the Town Hall area.

Bottom: Chester's inner ring road was all 'bright, shiny and new' when this photograph was taken in 1966, and although the camera has caught a quiet moment, there is no doubt that pressure from 'through' traffic was now off the central streets. Dual carriageways and double yellow lines have become commonplace, but in the Chester of 1966 this view represented the culmination of plans which, in one form or another, had been on the drawing board since 1945. As with so much else in Chester, the old is never very far from the new, and a few steps to the left from the dual carriageway takes you back something like 200 years. King's Buildings is a well restored Georgian terrace of 1776, and a walk up King Street to its junction with Northgate would bring you to the Pied Bull, an inn whose eighteenth century frontage is one of the newer bits! The two cars on view are a Morris Oxford, approaching the camera, and a Morris Minor, heading inwards from St Martin's Gate. Some readers who learned to drive around this time may have fond recollections of making their first 'hiccoughing' attempts in a car such as this. Even the registration plate - 7861 N - would be worth 'a bob or two' now.

GETTING AWAY FROM IT ALL

Britain's first stretch of motorway was not, as is popularly believed, the M1. The eight-and-a-quarter miles long Preston Bypass - later part of the M6 - was opened by Prime Minister Harold Macmillan in December 1958.

Vast swathes were cut through the outskirts of towns as ring roads were built to take traffic away from town centres. A network of motorways speeded the average journey, and by the end of the 20th century Britain had more than 2,000 miles of motorway.

Post-war prosperity meant that more families could aspire to that badge of one-upmanship - a new car. Hot off the production line in 1959 was the Mini - destined to become the 1960s 'car of the decade'.

The long sweep of the inner ring road from the Northgate round-about to St Martin's Gate, in the bottom right-hand corner, dominates this aerial view. From the volume of contractors' vehicles and materials on the embryo roundabout, and along St Martin's Way, it is clear that construction is still in progress, dating the photograph to 1965-6. An older form of transport takes pride of place on the right-hand side as the course of the Shropshire Union Canal can be traced, following the line

of the old city wall from top to bottom of the photograph. It began life as the Chester Canal in 1779 and became the Shropshire Union in 1833 when it was linked to the Trent and Mersey Canal at Middlewich. At the very bottom, close to the railway line, the beginning of a 'staircase' of three locks can be seen. These were built by the famous canal engineer,

Thomas Telford, and drop the canal almost to the level of the River Dee. The top stretch of the Canal is crossed by Northgate, and just below this is the tiny Bridge of Sighs, once used by prisoners from the old Northgate Gaol, who had been condemned to death. The imposing building to the left is the former Bluecoat School built in 1717.

On the move

Whatever happened to winters? Chester is not known as one of Britain's snowiest spots, but the 'white outs' used to occur from time to time, more so than they do today. The style of the bus suggests a wintry scene in the 1950s, and no doubt the miserable and frozen bus queue near the Odeon in Northgate Street was glad of the sight of it - unless it was stuck! A mention of global warming would have brought a hollow laugh from these poor souls, and probably a cry of 'the sooner the better'. Adversity brings people together, however, and they probably chatted to each other more freely than usual. There is an old saying about 'an ill wind', and the proprietor of Northern Raincoats, right opposite the bus queue, could hardly have been complaining about the blizzard. Of course, it all thaws away in the end, and it doesn't seem so many years ago that you could watch great swathes of snow suddenly slide off the slates and shutter down to the pavement in a great cascade. What a delight to children this was, but nowadays centrally heated homes tend to melt the snow on the roof before it has time to accumulate, and so that satisfying spectacle has largely gone.

Above: It is the two buses that provide the main focus for this 1944 shot as they head past the junction of Eastgate Street and St Werburgh Street. It is odd to think of these as 'museum pieces', and yet they do belong to another age, with their open platforms and the conductor in charge, money pouch slung across one shoulder and ticket machine across the other. It would probably surprise us all to realise just how many years ago it was that conductors became generally redundant, and 'Pay as you enter' became part of our lives. The advertisements on these 1944 buses may summon up memories for some Cestrians. Perhaps you had a fireplace that came from Moore & Brock Ltd, or perhaps you remember the Tamil Cafe on St Werburgh Street. This was situated right next to the very striking Martin's Bank building (later Barclays) which is visible in the background, to the right. Perhaps most evocative of all is the Bisto advertisement. You can instantly picture those Bisto Kids, heads held high in bliss as delicious smells waft up their noses! The trouble for the 1944 housewife was that the Bisto may have been plentiful, but the meat was scarce. Wartime rationing saw to that - unless the 'black market' came to your aid.

Above right: Excavating equipment, workmen and the concrete supports of a flyover present an all too familiar sight in images of the 1960s. In common with the rest of Britain, Chester faced increasing problems as the rising numbers of vehicles after World War II began to clog up city centres. Traffic from the east and north-east heading for Wales, had to go right through the heart of Chester in order to get to Grosvenor Bridge across the Dee. It wasn't simply a matter of congestion and delays, awareness began to grow too of the potential health hazards to pedestrians from the dangerous 'cocktail' of fumes hanging in the air. As far back as 1945 plans were being considered for an inner ring road for 'through' traffic. It took some time to 'grasp the nettle', for inevitably it would mean the destruction of some of Chester's rich heritage, but by the 1960s it was felt that traffic was choking the life out of the city, and something just had to be done. The photograph shows the breaching of the city walls from the direction of Canal Street in December 1964, whilst the concrete supports seem to advance ominously towards the houses in front of them. Parts of the old Roman Fortress were found during this operation.

Below: The progress of the inner ring road by February 1965 is shown in this photograph, as it makes a rather graceful curve over the railway lines towards the Northgate roundabout by the church. There is the usual clutter of contractors' materials and vehicles, including a Ford Anglia, a well remembered car of that era. This particular stretch of the inner ring road was named St Martin's Way, and a continuation off the bottom of the photograph would show it arriving at St Martin's Gate. The latter was the point where the breach in the old city walls had been made in late 1964. The Gate was completed and named early in 1966, after the Council had rejected suggestions to call it Winston Churchill Gate. At a public meeting in December 1964 the Consultant Architect to the scheme had described it as a 'Twenty-Five Year Plan for Chester'. No matter how great the necessity, however, such schemes always mean sacrifices for some. After living on the quiet Garden Lane for 27 years, Mr P Ratcliffe and his wife suddenly had to cope with traffic roaring past close to their bedroom windows. Their next door neighbour, Miss E Williamson, had watched her home being built, and now she had to watch it being demolished - after 55 years.

> *During the breach of the City walls to make way for the ring road, parts of the original Roman fortress were uncovered*

An absolutely fascinating array of building styles are represented in this view of the Market Square, dating from the late 1960s or early 1970s. Judging by the rectangular glass and concrete structure in the background, to the left of the Town Hall, the market redevelopment scheme of

that time is more or less in place. Inevitably, the utilitarian style of the 1960s creation suffers in comparison with the flamboyance of the Town Hall, built exactly 100 years before. This magnificent Gothic structure, with its alternate bands of red and grey sandstone, boasts a central tower 160 feet in height and some

superb carved stonework. Opened by Edward, Prince of Wales in 1869 the Town Hall seems to express all the confidence and self-belief of that Victorian age. It was designed by William Henry Lynn of Belfast. Wedged between the Coach and Horses and the Shropshire Arms, both exponents of the 'black and white revival' style, is the striking Edwardian facade of the City Library. It was converted in the late 1970s from the Westminster Coach and Motor Car Works, whose name can clearly be seen on the central arch at the top. To complete the picture, the fluted brickwork of the Odeon Cinema, built in 1936, is just visible to the far right.

*C*hester has many charms, not least the River Dee, and on a hot summer's day there is little to beat simply 'messing about on the river'. It's not so bad in winter too, and in this 1962 scene the leafless appearance of the trees gives the clue that this is the season. The people strolling along The Groves, Chester's well-known riverside promenade, are pretty warmly clad, and it might be significant that a couple walking away from the refreshment kiosk have chosen candy floss rather than ice-cream! Nevertheless, lots of hardy souls have taken to the boats, a number of which can be seen dotted about in the area of the suspension bridge. The graceful looking Queen's Park Bridge was opened in 1923 to replace the earlier bridge of 1852. This latter had been built to link the new suburb of Queen's Park, south of the river, with the city itself. Regattas have been held on the Dee since the early nineteenth century and pleasure boats ply the river. However, the toddler in the foreground is enjoying one of the simplest pleasures of all - feeding the swans. Of course, rivers can be associated with work too, and in the seventeenth century the river drove 11 waterwheels to power the Dee Mills.

At leisure

Obviously this is a special event for both adults and children at the City Mission in October 1958, for everyone is in their 'Sunday best', and the little girl at the front is proudly holding a large bouquet of flowers. The event was, in fact, 'First Sunday', which sounds like an anniversary of some sort, possibly of the founding of the Mission. If this was the case, then there was every reason for celebration, for in 1958 the Crook Street City Mission had a proud record of 114 years of spreading the Christian gospel. Not only this, it was practical Christianity in action, with the

emphasis on looking after the welfare of anyone in need, young or old. Annual excursions to the seaside or countryside proved especially popular with the young. This photograph is of unusual interest because on the left, starting with the two boys in bow ties, there are three sets of twins. Next to them is a girl with a striped scarf, and her sister peeps over her shoulder. Next again are two slightly older girls in dark coats, one wearing glasses. The City Mission spent its last year at Crook Street in 1958, for it then moved to better premises at the former Bishop Graham's School on Princess Street.

Chester Library

Both pictures: Is this Chester or Manchester? These images from the mid-1960s evoke the atmosphere of a northern industrial city, in true Coronation Street style, but they belong to Chester. Quite understandably, they are not the kind of photographs that appear in guide books, for it is the 'black and white' Chester that appeals to prospective visitors. Nevertheless, such streets were just as much a part of the city for those Cestrians who lived there, and it is as well that some photographer took these unglamorous shots - just for the record. The first picture *(right)* shows a rather long and bleak shot, possibly of Victor Street, in January 1966, with the dustbins lined up in an orderly fashion. These were the days before the black plastic bags, or the plastic bins for that matter, and the rubbish was tipped straight into the dustcart. What the lady on the doorstep was looking for we shall never know. Perhaps she was just taking the air. Oulton Place from George Street, looking towards St Anne's Street, is the subject of the second photograph *(top)*. This is a more lively scene, and the old car is perhaps misleading, for the motor-bike and moped at bottom left give it more of a 1960s feel.

Chester Library

Such areas are much altered now. Some streets were completely swept away in clearance schemes, or to make way for ring roads and relief roads. In other cases, parts of streets remained and have benefited from later improvement schemes, so that houses that were once always under the threat of the bulldozer have become 'character' Victorian residences. All growing cities have had housing problems, and Chester is no exception. The first council houses in the city were built in 1901 at Towerfields, at rents of around two shillings (10p) per week. Many slums existed along Foregate Street and in the area behind the Town Hall. Clearance schemes in the 1930s brought about their demolition, and people were resettled on suburban council estates such as those at Buddicom Park, Handbridge and Lache. After World War II there was a move towards creating completely self-contained townships, such as Blacon and Newton Hall. Mistakes were made, of course, and Chester did not escape the craze for tower blocks which afflicted the nation in the 1960s, often with disastrous social consequences. It is clear too that much basically sound property was bulldozed nationwide in the 1960s, and since then the trend has been towards the much more cost-effective process of 'improvement' rather than demolition.

Both pictures: Ordinary people on Foregate Street, caught perhaps at random by the camera, provide the focus for these two photographs. The first one *(bottom)* shows one D Paddock, who may well be aware of the camera. The fashions of the lady herself, and those around her, speak very much of the 1940s, as does the automobile. Also, there is a suggestion of men in uniform in the background. The lady in the fur coat has plenty to contend with, for not only is she pushing a pram, but she also has two youngsters 'in tow'. One of them is being held in check, however, by that very useful aid to infant control - a pair of reins. The second picture *(below)* also features a Paddock, this time a Mrs E Paddock, to the left of the group of three, but it is not known if she is a relation of

D Paddock. Then comes Mrs E Hughes, accompanied by R Hughes. The setting is again Foregate Street, this time around 1950. There is less opportunity for fashion spotting, but it is noticeable that the boy is wearing short trousers, and would be expected to do so for another few years yet. His gaberdine type raincoat is also a mark of the times, and many boys around 1950 would have topped it all off with a cap. How on earth would modern day youngsters, with their insistence on brand names and image, have coped with all that? As parents know to their cost, the 'right' style of trainers, for example, can take on life or death significance!

This is perhaps the keynote of these photographs - that in both cases this was an age of austerity. The one from the 1940s may have been taken at a time when wartime rationing was still in full force, with 66 clothes coupons for the entire year. To speak of 1940s fashions may rekindle memories in some readers' minds of wartime when clothing had to be 'fashioned', literally, from whatever was available. To save on materials and manpower, Utility Clothing had to be made, lacking embroidery and trimming, and with limited pleats, seams and buttonholes. Rationing was only gradually dismantled after World War II, and some would still be in existence around 1950, the date of the group photograph. The fashion industry for the young lay a few years ahead! As for Foregate Street itself, what would our shoppers of over 50 years ago have made of some of the icons of the modern age to be found there now, such as McDonalds, the Virgin Megastore and the Mobile Phone Shop?

M ilitary training and bloody combat would probably have been very far away from the minds of the people relaxing in the sunshine in these pleasant gardens alongside Little St John Street in 1958. However, whether they knew it or not, this little oasis of tranquillity had once formed part of Chester's Roman Amphitheatre, and some 1800 years earlier the air might well have been full of the noise of clashing weapons as legionaries trained or gladiators fought. The Amphitheatre had been discovered in 1928, and the partly demolished St John's House, formerly used as offices by the Cheshire County Council, was an indicator that more excavations were to begin in 1959. The demolition was to allow the City Corporation to re-align Little St John Street, which skirted one of the walls of the Amphitheatre. The large building to the right of St John's House was then the Grosvenor St John's School, and is now the Chester Visitor Centre. The imminent excavations, undertaken by the Ministry of Works, aimed to uncover the northern half of an arena which had seating for 7000 people, the largest stone one in Britain. No doubt it was packed on public holidays to witness some of the bloodier Roman entertainments, a far cry from the peaceful gardens, which also disappeared during the excavations.

Events & occasions

Either it is a very hot July day, or the gentleman on the left has taken his hat off in deference to the Duke of Westminster, who walks on the right of the picture. He is accompanying the Mayor, Alderman Miss Mary Heaney, on the occasion of the official opening of the Bridge Street Improvement Scheme in 1964. The Turog sign on the building in the rear almost literally gives a flavour of that era. The 1960s began the great age of modern tourism for Britons as car ownership increased hugely. The historic and visual attractions of Chester gave the city a headstart in attracting visitors, but it was felt by some that more could be done to highlight the charms and unique features of the city centre streets. The first scheme was a combined effort by the Civic Trust, the City Council and the Bridge Street Traders' Committee, headed by Mr John Welsby. The task was not easy because of the architecture of the Rows, but it included some repainting, some new signs and expert treatment to expose fine carvings and designs. A lighting scheme was devised so that at night the street lights illuminated the buildings, and both St Peters and St Michaels were floodlit. Overall the scheme brought much acclaim.

Chester Library

King George V and Queen Mary made several visits to Chester and district both as Prince and Princess of Wales and as reigning monarchs. The photograph, although undated, suggests that this occasion was the visit of the King and Queen to open an extension to the Royal Infirmary in 1914. The dress of the crowds seems to fit that era, as do the nurses' uniforms. An eager throng has gathered to witness what was undoubtedly a memorable and colourful spectacle. George V can be seen in the centre, inspecting two immaculately turned out lines of soldiers. A cavalry party faces the reception pavilion which carries the royal coat-

of-arms and the insignia of both George and Mary. Open-top carriages stand close by. The crowds of patriotic onlookers filling the square in the foreground must have been keen to get a closer view, but they seem to be exercising self-restraint without the aid of police or barriers. Such a grand spectacle was absent for the next royal visit to Chester, in 1917. After three years of the appalling slaughter of World War I the mood was subdued as King George and Queen Mary visited munitions factories, and also wounded soldiers convalescing in Chester Castle. Official 'pomp and circumstance' was banned - by royal order.

Bridge Street was packed with humanity to give an enthusiastic welcome to the royal cavalcade on the occasion of the visit of Princess Elizabeth in April 1951. Clearly the pressure of the crowds was too much, and the police simply had to let the people spill onto the road, leaving only a narrow corridor for the vehicles to sweep up. The famous Chester Rows were put to good use as viewing platforms, and the photograph shows people clinging onto every vantage point, right up to the roofs. Princess Elizabeth had arrived at the railway station at 9 30 am, to be greeted by the Lord-Lieutenant of Cheshire, Lord Leverhulme and the Mayor, Alderman PH Lawson. The main purpose of the visit was to attend a 'passing-out'

parade of officer cadets at Eaton Hall. The Princess took the salute as 400 cadets smartly marched past on the polo ground, accompanied by the band of the Welsh Guards. Lunch at Eaton Hall was organised by Bollands of Chester, who had arranged for fresh strawberries to be flown from France. Princess Elizabeth's return journey to Chester was marked by more patriotic scenes on the street. Apart from anything else, the visit provided a welcome spot of colour in the drab post-war austerity years.

ROYAL WATCH

The talking point of the early 1930s was the affair of the Prince of Wales, later King Edward VIII, and American divorcee Wallis Simpson. Faced with a choice, Edward gave up his throne to marry her. His Nazi sympathies were kept strictly under wraps at the time.

By the end of World War II, the 19-year-old Princess Elizabeth and Lieutenant Philip Mountbatten RN were already in love. The couple's wedding on 20th November 1947 was a glittering occasion - the first royal pageantry since before the war.

King George VI's health had been causing problems since 1948, when he developed thrombosis. In 1951 the King - always a heavy smoker - became ill again, and he was found to be suffering from lung cancer. He died in the early hours of 6th February 1952.

Princess Margaret's announcement in 1960 that she was to wed photographer Antony Armstrong-Jones brought pleasure to many who had sympathised when she ended her relationship with Peter Townsend in 1955. Her marriage to Lord Snowdon itself ended in 1978.

Left: It's a damp day in October 1949, and the union jacks hang a little limply from the buildings, but there is no doubting the enthusiasm of the crowds clustered densely around the Eastgate. The occasion was the visit of Queen Elizabeth, later the Queen Mother, and astonishingly she was already a grandmother by this point, over 50 years ago! The royal train had been due at the General Station at 9 30 am, and a glance at the Eastgate Clock will show that everything was on schedule. Having greeted the royal party at the station, the Mayor and Mayoress of Chester, Mr and Mrs Bert Reynolds, accompanied the Queen throughout her visit, as did Viscount and Viscountess Leverhulme. Queen Elizabeth commented on the beauty of Chester, although this was not a sightseeing visit. The main purpose was an inspection by the Queen of the officers and men of the Queen's Bays Regiment at the Dale, Upton-by Chester. The beautiful Eastgate Clock, under which the royal cavalcade is just passing, was designed by John Douglas, and a Handbridge blacksmith created the ornamental frame. Although intended for Queen Victoria's Diamond Jubilee in 1897, it was not actually in position until 1899, and so the clock's 50th anniversary just about coincided with this visit.

By the time the Queen Mother visited Chester in 1949, she was already a grandmother!

Below: The military neatness and straightness of the two lines of nurses must have been much to the taste of Colonel CW Marsden, pictured at the side of Queen Elizabeth II. The occasion was the visit of Her Majesty and the Duke of Edinburgh to Chester in July 1957, and the itinerary included this visit to the Royal Infirmary. A great deal of washing, starching, ironing, and polishing of shoes contributed to the immaculate appearance of the nurses, but no doubt it was worthwhile. After all, how many of them would ever have the chance to be so close to a monarch again? The royal arrival received a hugely enthusiastic and patriotic welcome from the crowds who packed the area around the Infirmary. The Matron, Miss E Brown, did the honours in escorting the Queen who showed especial interest in the children's ward. Before leaving the Infirmary, the Queen presented two signed photographs of herself and the Duke of Edinburgh to the Outpatients Department. Another part of the royal itinerary that day was to formally open the new County Hall. At the ceremony the Queen was presented with a silver cigarette case by Lowe and Sons of Bridge Street - an echo of the two George II tumblers which they had presented on the occasion of her visit as Princess Elizabeth in 1951.

Shopping spree

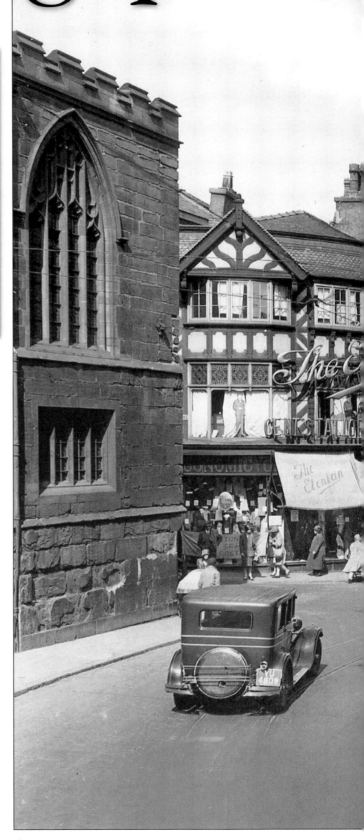

> From 1506 to 1803 the City Fathers ruled Chester from the Pentice, a timber framed building which adjoined the church

It is difficult to know which is the most eye-catching here - the wonderful old cars, the elegant architecture or the arresting female fashions. The historic heart of Chester is captured in this shot looking down Eastgate from the Cross, and which probably dates back to the 1920s. Of course, this is 'only yesterday' in terms of the recorded history of Chester and the important, sometimes turbulent, events witnessed at this spot. The Romans had their administrative headquarters on the site now occupied by St Peter's Church, visible on the far left, and this in turn may well have been founded as early as 907 AD by Ethelfleda, Countess of Mercia. From 1506 to 1803 the City Fathers ruled Chester from the Pentice, a timber-framed building which adjoined the Church. Nearby, some of the recipients of their justice stood unhappily in the Pillory. The Cross was the scene of bull-baiting and riots, but also happier events, such as in 1685 when the water conduit at the Pentice was filled with wine to celebrate the bringing of Charles II's charter to the city. However, history is as much about continuity as change, and a visit to those famous steps at the far right of the photograph would still find Walton the jewellers trading there.

Chester Archives: ref CH 1145

Above: The US serviceman who photographed this Eastgate Street scene in 1944, Robert Astrella, may well have been taken by the nice contrast in architectural styles displayed by the Westminster (formerly Parr's) Bank to the right and the seemingly older exteriors on view. Indeed the Tudor Cafe appears to be a very appropriate name for a building which has such an 'olde worlde' flavour. It may or may not have come as a surprise to Mr Astrella that the bank building was probably the older one, built in Classical style by George Williams in 1859-60, and so very distinctive with its Corinthian columns. The Tudor Cafe, in common with many of Chester's 'black and white' buildings, was likely to have been a product of late Victorian revivalism - a mock Renaissance effect achieved by nailing painted boards to brick. It would be interesting to know what was on offer at the Tudor Cafe in 1944, for strict rationing had been in force since 1940, and perhaps coupons were needed even for a cup of tea. A better bet might have been the British Restaurant in Northgate Street. Sponsored by the government, with the aim of catering mainly for war industry workers, anyone could get an 'off-ration' meal at a British Restaurant for around one shilling (5p).

Right: This was a problem that was only going to get worse. The cyclists in this 1951 view of Eastgate Street have plenty of time to admire the line of sturdy 1940s saloon cars as they seek a chink of space to squeeze through. Even the pedestrian at the bottom right-hand corner seems trapped. This may well have all the appearance of local rush hour traffic, but in 1951 the centre of Chester had also to contend with through traffic from the east and north-east heading for Wales. This 'bottleneck' effect was compounded by the growth of private car ownership and commercial road transport in the two decades after World War II, until the inner ring road scheme of the 1960s considerably relieved the problem. It is not simply the cars that betray the fact that this little scene took place the best part of half a century ago. There is no sign of any cycling gear on these young men apart from the cycle clips to hold in the baggy trousers of the day. Also the Fifty Shilling Tailors was a well-known retailing chain of the day, but if that referred to a complete suit, well £2.50 would just about buy a pair of socks today!

MEADOW

PEARL ASSURANCE COMPANY

PEARL

THE FIFTY SHILLING TAILORS

KXF 829

Anyone wandering down Bridge Street from its junction with Eastgate Street will find plenty of interest. If inscriptions are your 'cup of tea' then you could start at the impressive building at the junction, the one housing Walton & Son, and find the city arms and motto, 'Antiqui Colant Antiquum Dierum'. In other words, 'Let the Ancients honour the Ancient of Days'. If that seems less than clear, there is a simpler one on the Art Gallery, towards the bottom of the street. The Gallery, richly decorated with Biblical messages and scenes, also has this simple inscription on it - 'To God, my King and my Country'. The Chester Heritage Centre, opened in 1975 on the theme of the city's history, is easy to spot, being housed in what was

formerly St Michael's Church, at the far right of the photograph. The latter was taken in the 1950s, and clearly a stroll down Bridge Street is easier in its present pedestrianised form than it was in those traffic-congested days. The Bridge Street Row East is well displayed in this shot, but apart from B Walton & Son, the trading names on view have disappeared. However, hidden within the arcades is a name which represents continuous business at the same shop since 1803 - that of Lowe & Sons, silversmiths.

THE POUND IN YOUR POCKET

In the 1920s and 30s meals were still being produced on the old kitchen range. Only the better-off could afford a gas cooker; in 1928 you would have to pay around £25 for the new appliance - around 17 weeks' wages.

Mars bars sold for 2d when they were first produced in 1932. Mars became the UK's best selling chocolate bar - and by the end of the 20th century (by that time costing 30 pence) around three million were eaten every day.

Wages were rising in the 1930s - but slowly. Two million were still unemployed. In 1939 rump steak cost 1/6d per lb, while pork sausages were 6d. Food, clothing and petrol rationing was introduced in 1940, allowing a weekly ration of a shilling's worth of meat.

Far fewer people spent their money on DIY in the 1930s and 40s. Wallpaper had to be trimmed with a pair of scissors, and paste was made with flour and water. Brilliant white paint - unknown before then - began to transform our homes in the mid 50s.

Things have certainly changed on Eastgate Street since this rather hectic scene was captured in August 1951. Cars, pedestrians and cyclists are slugging it out, although the belisha beacon controlled crossing and the white-sleeved policeman on point duty are helping to ensure that it is not total anarchy. The rise of mass car ownership from the 1960s only aggravated such problems until ring roads and pedestrianisation produced a calmer atmosphere. Another change lies in the shop names on view. Older readers may remember the days when HL Gerry was a dispensing pharmacist, or you could get measured for a suit at John Smith & Son the

tailors. J Collinson & Son and Valstar are also names which stand out, but with the exception of Jaeger House, to the left, it all seems pretty unfamiliar to the modern eye. Commercial giants such as Cheltenham and Gloucester, the Edinburgh Woollen Mill and Waterstones dominate this particular view today. The line of rabbits hanging from the gallery above the butcher's shop draws attention to the Rows, and how different again this scene would have been about 350 years ago. The houses above the galleries protruded so far into the street that they almost touched each other, as did the open stalls or shops upon which they rested. More congestion!

Chester Library

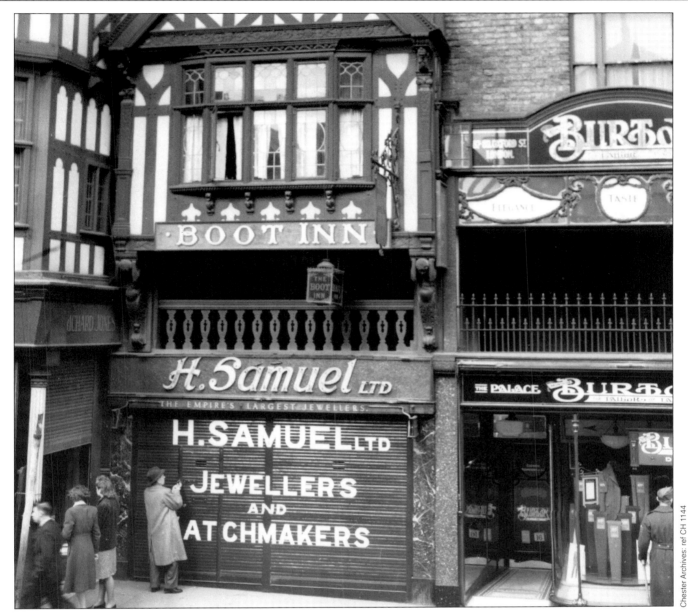

Left: The distinctive pair of spectacles attached to the balustrade above the sign for Siddall the opticians is an eye-catching device. More curious than this, however, is the fact that the business combined optical work with making umbrellas in 1948, and the connection between the two is difficult to fathom out. The giant pair of glasses is an echo of Medieval times, when the famous Chester Rows were often named after the business conducted there, so that there was a Shoemakers Row and Ironmongers Row, along with the very evocative Pepper Alley and Fish Shambles. Not only this, giant symbols were often hung in prominent positions to illustrate the products for sale. The photograph shows the Bridge Street Row to good effect, and one can imagine the bustle of activity up the ladders and along the narrow walkways of the old Medieval Rows. By the seventeenth century the stalls extended so far into the streets, from both sides, as almost to block them, and a law of 1673 insisted that the 'stallboards' had to be made with hinges so that they could be 'folded up at night'. The Rows have changed much since then, as have all the shop names on this photograph bar one. Siddall the opticians still trade at this spot in Chester.

Above: The man in charge of shuttering and padlocking H Samuel Ltd, Jewellers and Watchmakers, is making a thorough job of it, and well he might. Such places can be vulnerable at the best of times, but in 1944 the streets of Chester were perhaps more restless places than they had been before the war. The figure looking in the window of Burtons, at far right, gives the clue. This was an American serviceman, and during World War II many British, Polish and American military personnel were stationed around Chester. This was good for business, but there were many complaints about drunken and disorderly behaviour in the normally sedate streets and public houses of the city. Another problem of quite a different nature was the fact that American servicemen always had plenty of money, and seemingly limitless supplies of wartime luxuries such as nylons and cigarettes. This made them very attractive to females, and it was little wonder that local males tended to grumble about the Americans being, 'over paid, over sexed and over here!' The name of H Samuel can still be found at Eastgate Street, as can that of the Boot Inn - a fine old hostelry first licensed in 1643.

The lower end of Bridge Street by night makes for an unusual shot in 1965, and perhaps something out of the ordinary has taken place if that is a police motor-cyclist who is talking to someone at far right. The road signs just below the bus stop, indicating destinations such as Manchester and North Wales, show that the inner ring road had not yet been completed, and that 'through' traffic still had to plough through the city centre streets. The photograph provides a good illustration of the Rows and the number of shops which can be packed into two levels. Some readers may well remember these 1965 names -

Lawleys, Quinceys, Sellers, Simpson's, Venables, Rentaset, Beachcomber Travel, Typewriter Exchange and the Chanticleer Restaurant. How many are still there today? Some very fine buildings are on view, and the very narrow one next to the bus stop is a genuine half-timbered seventeenth century survivor. The tower of St Michael's Church is very visible against the night sky. Originally a Medieval foundation, the church was rebuilt in 1582 and once again by James Harrison of Chester between 1849 and 1851. It became redundant as a Church in 1972, but reopened as the Chester Heritage Centre in 1975, the first one of its kind in Britain.

This Spring Buying Event at the Grosvenor Precinct, around 1966, certainly seems to be generating a lot of interest as visitors cluster around the central feature. Whatever it was, it must have been worth seeing, for one mum is about to lift her youngster up to get a better view. It has to be admitted, however, that the majority of the enthusiasts are female, and the old gentleman sitting down at far left seems to be indicating that he has had enough already! We are very familiar with large shopping plazas now, and so it is perhaps difficult to remember the excitement which surrounded the opening of the Grosvenor Precinct

in November 1965, the first one of its scale in Chester. Totally covered, with controlled indoor temperatures and multi-storey car parking, the Grosvenor-Laing development seemed to be the very epitome of modern-day shopping. The Piazza was superbly decorated for the featured event, possibly on an Italian theme. However, the presence of the Cellini Boutique and the Vallerina Stocking Bar may have just been coincidental. The speciality of Cellini was ladies' handbags, ranging in price from 26 shillings (£1.30) to crocodile ones at £130. Apparently, Italian bead handbags were very popular at the time. Remember those?

At work

Just prior to the second world war, the Anchor Motor Company had premises at Pepper Street and Grosvenor Street, with repair workshops at Park Street. The last named was probably the location for this scene, once the energies of the company had been thrown totally into aircraft production for the war effort. Six women are busily scraping the fabric off used wings to prepare for the making of new ones. Scores of wing frames are stacked at the back and on shelves. Aircraft work went on elsewhere in and around Chester at this time. The firm of Dixon-Bate in Tarvin Road made aircraft parts, and also developed special airborne trolleys. After 'D'-Day, in June 1944, parachute forces used these trolleys to carry ammunition, stores and even the wounded. At nearby Broughton, the Vickers-Armstrong factory built 5540 Wellington bombers, along with some Lancasters and Lincolns. All the workers on the ground must have been tremendously cheered in August 1940 at the news that three training instructors from RAF Hawarden had used their Spitfires to bring down a Heinkel III German bomber at Sealand.

Chester Archives: ref CH 1836

The sweet smell of success!

The bakers and confectionery company, Weinholt's of Chester, was founded in 1953 by Frank Weinholt. However, the history of the family trade can actually be traced back some 130 years.

Indeed it was Frank's great grandfather, Ferdinand Wienholdt, in the years before the family name was changed, who became the first member of the family to develop an expertise in the confectionery trade. In the year 1870, Ferdinand opened a confectioners shop in Market Street in Manchester. It was from here that Ferdinand developed his expertise in Danish pastries. The plate size Danish pastries were not to Mancunians' liking and by cutting these into slices were better accepted - so was created the vanilla slice.

Ferdinand's son, August, was born in 1874 and was soon to inherit his father's love of bakery and become the second generation of Wienholt's to work in the confectionery trade. In 1899, August came to Chester in order to train the staff in Cottles, a high class confectionery business based in Bridge Street. After completing this task he opened his own business, The Premier Cafe in Cheadle, Cheshire.

August's son, Carl, also inherited his father's and grandfather's love of all things edible. Before he went into business within the food industry however, he implemented a change that was to be more far reaching in the family's history than his business venture as a fish fryer. The advent of the first world war saw Carl going off to serve his country in the South Lancashire Regiment, joining up at Chester Castle at the age of sixteen. It also saw Carl changing the family name from Wienholdt to Weinholt in an attempt to Anglicise it, the reason being that he was fighting against Germany and he thought it wrong that he should have a German sounding name.

Above: *An artists' impression of the firm's family tree.*
Below: *John's great-grandfather, August Wienholdt with his wife and staff at the Premier Café during the 1920s.*

The altered family name was upheld by the following generations of Weinholt's. Indeed Carl's son, Frank, founded the present business under this name in 1953. Like his grandfather before him, Frank developed an expertise in the industry. He studied at the bakery department of Denbighshire College, Wrexham and then gained experience working for his uncles, Frank and George, before opening a small bakery and shop in Handbridge, Chester. With the help of his wife, Irene and his sister, Margaret, Frank's business began to flourish. It was not long before the business outgrew its premises and was able to acquire the premises on either side, enabling the shop to be extended and the bakery to be transferred to a modern building at the rear of the shop.

Frank's son, John had shown a keen interest in the business from the early age of eight when he had had to stand on a box of fat in order to reach the bakery table! This interest was developed when, after obtaining his O Levels, he studied at Hollins College in Manchester. Here, he won an award for the best student of a six months scholarship for craft study in Switzerland. Indeed, after gaining experience in Europe he joined the family business in 1974 and was responsible for introducing bread and the use of chocolate

Top: Eliza Moore (second from right), who worked all her working life for three generations of Weinholts, all shown on this picture. Above: Frank with the Royal cake pictured with Robert Vickers (left) and Kelvin Davies (right). Right: Thankyou letter from the palace.

in what was, up until then, a confectionery only firm.

Only two years after joining the business, John was able to play a part in the opening of a second shop at the Bache in Upton, Chester. This shop also enjoyed a steady success and John's sister, Ann joined the Chocolate Department after gaining a Diploma in Food Technology from Manchester Polytechnic.

The year 1981 was a special one in the history of the firm. It was in this year that Weinholt's was invited to present a cake for the wedding of H R H Prince Charles and Lady Diana Spencer. The four tier cake was eventually completed after a total of 800 working hours!

The year 1984 was also landmark year for Weinholt's. In this year the firm opened a city centre shop at Watergate Street. The shop was too large for just a cake shop and so Ann came up with the idea of opening a coffee lounge at the rear which in fact, she managed full time until 1992. Following the success of this coffee lounge another was opened at Upton's small bakery and all production was moved to the further extended original bakery at Handbridge.

In 1992 John, successfully opened a second city centre shop and coffee lounge in Northgate Street. In the following year - Weinholt's 40th anniversary - John was made senior partner of his family's business. Throughout his early career John won many craft prizes and a scholarship to work in bakery in Switzerland. John maintained the family connection with the British Confectioners Association and is currently on the committee responsible for craft presentation. His father Frank, having served two years as Chairman and four years as President, has been made an Honorary Member for life.

John's sisters, Ann, Karen and Jane have all contributed their expertise to the firm. Indeed, with their help and the service of a very loyal staff, John is hoping to continue providing a quality service to the people of Chester and in doing so, maintain the sweet smell of success unique to the Weinholt family confectionery and bakery business.

Both pictures: If air power was the key to victory in World War II, then these workers at the Anchor Motor Company, Chester, were doing what they could to get those planes made. The two women working at the front end of the cockpit *(right)* look to be engaged in some complex technical work. Even if it soon became routine to them , there was no doubting its importance to Britain's war effort. The second photograph *(below)* shows the interior of the cockpit from the rear. If anything, it all looks more complicated than ever, but this would have been the view for part of the aircrew - the brave men who flew these planes. The male worker looking closely at the paperwork attached to the side of the aircraft is probably checking out the work to be done and the deadline for completion. Speed was of the essence, for these pictures were taken in 1939, a year during which frantic efforts were being made to catch up with Germany's 'Luftwaffe' in terms of numbers. The Anchor Motor Company, established in the early 1920s in Park Street, was one of many motor engineering firms nationwide which found that its skills and machinery could be adapted to national needs.

The coming of war on September 3rd 1939 meant radical changes in all walks of life, not simply on the factory floor. The government feared massive casualties from the bombing of cities, and plans to evacuate 2,500,000 children from vulnerable industrial areas were put into operation. Chester received a batch of evacuees instantly, from Liverpool. Gas masks had been distributed before the outbreak of war, and civilians were instructed that they must take them everywhere. Among the many public air raid shelters in Chester were those in the basements of Blossoms Hotel in Foregate Street and St Michael's Arcade in Bridge Street. The vaults of the Oddfellows Hall, and the crypt of St John's Church in Vicars Lane, served the same purpose. Six months before the war began, family shelters for gardens, known as Anderson Shelters, were being turned out at a rate of 80,000 a week. What really brought home to people that a war was on was the total blackout after sunset imposed by the government. No street lights were permitted, and prowling air raid wardens ensured that no chinks of light escaped from houses. The aeroplanes being made at the Anchor Motor Company would play their part in making the enemy know that there was a war on, too.

Chester Archives: ref CH 1806

Quality made to measure

The year 1952 was not the most advantageous one in which to establish a new business. It was in this year however, with rationing still in progress, that the Chester based business, Montgomery Tomlinson Limited, first came into existence.

The marriage of Agnes Montgomery to Arthur Tomlinson was not only an important event for the couple themselves, but was also a significant one in the history of Montgomery Tomlinson Limited. Indeed, without this union the business would not have been founded. When the couple married, Arthur was busy gathering valuable business experience working as an Area Manager for the tie company, Tootal Broadhurst Lee. However, Agnes' ambitions for her husband reached further than this and she encouraged him to set up his own business. It was then, with Agnes' encouragement and help, that Arthur set up a haberdashery business which was to evolve into the family soft furnishing business, Montgomery Tomlinson Limited.

Agnes and Arthur lived in a rented house. Their landlord refused to sell it to them, so, they were forced to look elsewhere for business premises. These premises were found in the shape of a one room property in Upper Northgate Street. It was from these premises that Monty and Tommy, as they were affectionately known, began trading in any kind of clothing or household goods that they could buy and then sell at a profit. This included anything, from plastic tablecloths to men's underwear!

Between them, the couple managed every aspect of the business including selling, administration, packaging, and delivery. Indeed, the sight of Tommy driving his old Armstrong-Siddeley picking up orders during the week, became a familiar one throughout North Wales. The couple's workload however, was eased at weekends as on Saturday mornings their young sons, Grahame and John, started to help out in the family business. Grahame still remembers parcelling up the orders, often for odd items and small amounts, piling them up in the old car and then, after a lunch of sandwiches and the contents of Thermos flasks made up by his mother, climbing into the back seat and

Below: The fleet in the 1980s. **Bottom:** *Grahame Tomlinson in the late 1960s in central Chester.*

had inherited his parents' entrepreneurial spirit and so, when he came out of the Army in 1957, he decided to set out on his own in an attempt to fulfil his ambitions. Grahame duly set off to London on his only means of transport - a scooter called Priscilla! Indeed, he used Priscilla for two years whilst in London and she now takes pride of place at the company's current premises. After driving 200 miles on Priscilla, Grahame made the audacious move of inter-rupting a furniture manufacturer's board meeting in order to announce that he was the man for the job of being their agent for the south. His audacity and enthusiasm paid off and he was given the job.

In 1959 the business moved to Falcon House. This property was an ex-townhouse that had belonged to the Duke of Westminster's family and amongst its many interesting features was a secret passageway, now safely blocked up, which led to the River Dee.

It was whilst working as a furniture agent that Grahame seized the opportunity to set up his own division of the

making the deliveries with the rest of the family. John later went on to become a doctor but Grahame, perhaps spurred on by his fond memories, went on to play a significant role within the family business, eventually becoming the Managing Director.

The burgeoning business began to flourish and Monty and Tommy were soon able to expand their stock. It was not long before they became agents for Rufflette tapes as well as selling ladies' and men's underwear and wholesale furnishing fabrics. By 1954, only two years after setting up in business, the couple were also able to move to larger and better premises in Northgate Street.

Their son Grahame made the decision not to join the family business in Chester. Grahame believed that there was not much money to be made in his parents' line of business. He

Above: *The premises at Saltney in the early 1970s.*
Top: *Montgomery's workroom in 1983 with the factory manager, Gill Bellis in the foreground.*
Right: *Grahame's parents, Arthur and Agnes Tomlinson with the staff in the late 1970s.*

family business. During the course of his work as an agent, Grahame walked into a furniture store in Holloway, North London. This seemingly mundane event was to shape the course of Montgomery Tomlinson Limited's history. On entering the store, Grahame made the astute perception that the furniture looked particularly attractive and comfortable because of the cushions arranged on them. On learning that the cushions were made by the shop assistant's wife, Grahame arranged a meeting with her. She told him that she had been sewing the cushions in her council flat. Grahame immediately recognised the opportunity for a successful business venture and took her and her husband into business with him, setting up in a small factory under the Montgomery Tomlinson name.

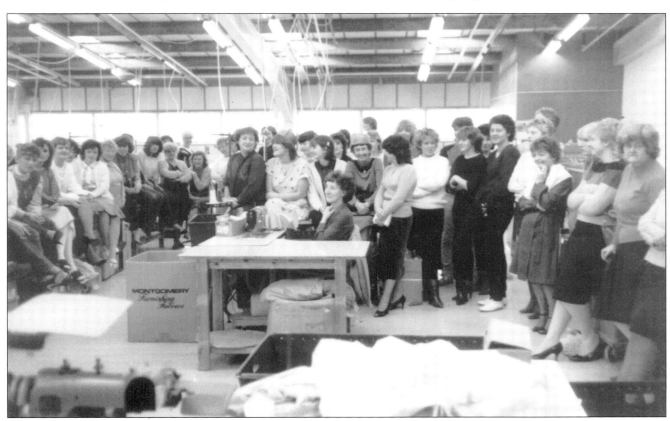

Grahame's new business, like his parents' before him, began to flourish. A major breakthrough for the fledgling business was the introduction of cushions made from fur fabric, inspired by a trip of Grahame's to Canada. The fur cushions had a screw-button centre, enabling the cover to be removed for cleaning, and soon big stores such as John Lewis and Debenhams became customers. Grahame worked hard to sell his product. Indeed, one day he pulled up outside the buying offices of a leading department store on Priscilla, next to a chauffeur driven Rover with the Sanderson rep inside. The men both raced

up the stairs to be first in line to see the buyer and luckily Grahame won the race and in turn, the contract!

Only a year after establishing the business it had become successful enough to be able to expand. As a result, in 1958, Grahame brought part of the business back to Chester. He negotiated with the Duke of Westminster's estate to rent Falcon House at £6 a week for 20 years and part of the premises, an area at the back, was used for making cushions. Grahame's mother Agnes had given her son considerable help in his new business when it was in London and had learned all about the manufacture of cushions. Therefore, when the business was brought to Chester, Monty insisted on forming a separate company so that she could establish her own product. Grahame agreed and Monty set to work starting at five in the morning, often working until eight at night, delivering cut fabric to the seamstresses she employed. Indeed, Monty carried on in this way from 1958 right up until 1964.

Business in Chester was thriving and it was not long before Grahame made the decision to sell the London venture in order to concentrate his efforts in Chester. By 1965 the business had grown to such an extent that Grahame decided to acquire a 'proper' factory in Saltney and shortly after-

Above: *The workroom in the late 1970s.*
Below: *The factory staff at a presentation in the late 70s.*

wards left Falcon House. It was in the Saltney factory during the 1960s that Montgomery Tomlinson Limited refined Michael Hadida's new 'Duplex' method of printing fabric on both sides and subsequently adopted it. This transformation in production methods meant that before long the main concentration of the business moved from cushions to furnishing fabrics.

It was during a trip to the United States of America that Grahame first learned of the idea of producing custom-made curtains. On his return to Britain, Grahame used his innovation once again to pioneer a new way of trading. He persuaded department stores to implement his made-to-measure gallery, shop-within-shop concept, in order to take orders for curtains which he would then make up in his factory. Dingles of Plymouth and Whittakers of Bolton were the first to take the plunge, but other stores, encouraged by this success, soon began to follow suit. Indeed today, Montgomery Tomlinson have over 100 of these shop-in shops and the company's flagship store in Chester is Browns.

Above: A view of the present Motgomery factory in the mid 1990s. Top: The board of directors with Alun Michael JP MP AM, First Secretary of the National Assembly for Wales at the opening of the new warehouse in November 1999. Right: A typical Montgomery concession. This one is in Debenhams of Plymouth.

The 1980s and 1990s saw the business expanding even further and indeed, becoming international, selling yardage to EU countries, the Middle East, and Australasia as well as exporting company designs to 25 countries world-wide. In 1999, a new 20000 square foot distribution warehouse was opened by Alun Michael, the First Secretary of the National Assembly for Wales to cater for the recent diversification into the ready-made market.

Today, Montgomery Tomlinson Limited occupies an 87000 square foot building which serves as the head office and factory for 600 retail outlets throughout the United Kingdom and the Republic of Ireland. The Company now employs 250 people at the Bretton site and a further 400 people as consultants in department stores throughout the country. Indeed, with the third generation of Tomlinsons - Grahame's son Paul - working for the business, Montgomery Tomlinson Limited is set to maintain its character as a successful family run business in the future.

There are plenty of cheerful faces at this wartime Christmas meal for the employees of the Anchor Motor Company. These were grim times, and perhaps Christmas involved no more than a couple of days break from making planes, but they were determined to make the best of it. All ages are represented on the photograph, but many young people are present, particularly women. This reflected the absence of most men of 'fighting age' on military duty, and the fact that women had swollen the ranks of the industrial workforce. In fact, during the second world war, the working population of Chester increased

from 5000 to 16000, and many of these were women who normally would have been at home. The decorative features of the Social Club are a mixture of the patriotic and the festive, large Union Jacks complementing the 'Merry Christmas' messages. The flowers provide a nice touch on the tables, and from the evidence of the bottles and glasses there has been plenty of liquid refreshment. Such events had to be enjoyed to the full, a brief release from eking out the miserly weekly allowances of some foodstuffs that were permitted by wartime rationing, eg two ounces (56 grammes) each of tea, butter and cheese and, incredibly, half an egg!

THE BUST TO BOOM YEARS

As men answered the call to military service in world war II, women took over their jobs - and proved their worth in driving, engineering, munitions, and 101 other traditionally male fields.

The country was in a bad way at the end of the war in 1945. Nazi bombs had destroyed railways, docks, factories and mills, and hundreds of homes lay in ruins. Britain had to borrow heavily - which meant increasing exports by 75 per cent.

The Labour government granted steel to motor manufacturers who would concentrate on cars for export. Building licences went to companies willing to open factories in high unemployment areas.

By the 1950s British economy was back on track. At its worst, unemployment reached only around 400,000. Ordinary working people could afford to buy the latest kitchen equipment, televisions - and a family car.

With munitions and war production workers working long hours, often on a seven day week, breaks were very welcome indeed. Hence these aircraft production workers at the Anchor Motor Company would be making full use of their lunch hour in the crowded canteen. Perhaps they are enjoying listening to 'Workers Playtime' broadcast through the tannoy system, or simply relaxing and chatting as they take in some nourishment. It is very noticeable that the great majority of those on

view are young women. The demands made by the armed services on manpower were so great that women had to fill the gap on the Home Front. Opportunities opened up for women to contribute to the war effort in a variety of ways. Some joined the women's auxiliary branches of the armed forces; some entered the Land Army; yet others contributed through voluntary Civil Defence work or the Women's Voluntary Service. The women who chose war work such as those featured here, may have found it gruelling, but it gave them some financial independence and the bonus of 'off ration' meals. The notice concerning tickets made sure that this privilege was limited to the legitimate workers. The sign 'Coffee Today' was , literally, a sign of the times. Clearly it was not an everyday event!

Taking stock of over 30 years of success

The year 1962 was the founding year of the turkey breeding company, British United Turkeys Limited, or BUT as it is known. It was in this year that three small turkey breeders got together in order to form the new company. However, the idea to form a company in Britain was actually conceived in the previous year by Rupert Chalmers Watson.

It was in the summer of 1961 that Rupert Chalmers Watson met two North American turkey producers, George Nicholas from the USA and Mac Cuddy from Canada, who visited Britain with a view to implementing his brainchild! They set about accomplishing this task by trying to find the most attractive company with whom to form a relationship. As a result of their research, discussions and meetings, the longstanding UK turkey businesses of Fenton Barns; John S. Lintern Limited; and Hockenhull Turkeys were amalgamated with Turkey Research and Development. Stock was exchanged between Britain and the USA. So, on August 1st 1962, British United Turkeys Limited was established.

The object of the newly formed company was to operate efficient, large scale, genetic programmes and to sell breeding stock on a franchise basis to breeders in the UK and Europe. Each of the founding companies were mostly well known as growers and processors. However, Fenton Barns and Hockenhull Turkeys had, for some years, been breeding turkeys and conducting their own genetic improvement programmes.

Despite this, the franchising of breeding stock was a new concept in the UK where breeders had traditionally been more or less totally integrated, running their own strain and often carrying right through to

*Left: Rupert Chalmers Watson. **Below:** Early incubators. **Bottom:** Nikita Khruschev with Keith Geddes in Kiev, 1964.*

the end product. The BUT approach proved to be successful.

The company's breeding operation continued to expand and gradually, the processing side was phased out at Hoppers Farm and Hockenhull. An entirely new production system was designed and built in Cheshire to ensure the future health status of the stock. The project consisted of setting up a network of 12 rearing sites and 10 laying farms, each of which would be filled and emptied in turn so that no health problems could build up. This unique system stood the test of time and proved to be a significant strategic decision in the history of the company. Indeed, it was probably one of the major factors responsible for BUT's continuing success in the 1970s and 1980s!

Above: *Early promotion.* **Top:** *John Lintern.*
Right: *The original Cheshire Hatchery in 1964.*

The BUT bird was the creation of Hugh Arnold who went on to run the company's breeding programme for over 30 years until he retired in 1995. Indeed, the bird and the new BUT approach launched the company on its path to success. A number of breeders were impressed with the BUT approach and became customers.

The company's first European customer was Moorgut Kartzfehn, Germany. In 1964, the company visited the Poultry Fair in Kiev with birds being inspected by Nikita Khruschev. BUT continued to build links to supply the Russian Turkey Industry. Sales were made to Italy, Spain and France and business developed in the UK.

BUT's initial products were the Large Bronze and Large White turkeys. However, by 1965 the demand for Bronze turkeys was virtually extinct and the company turned its efforts over to offering white breeding stock in large and medium sizes called, the Triple 6 and the Triple 5! By the year 1967, the company made the decision to start to develop new strains of turkeys and with this in mind, incorporated Richard Lawrence's farms at Hermitage and Alvaston into BUT. In doing so, Richard became a Director of the

company. Mo Hawkins was appointed to the board to focus on the commercial development of the company and Hugh Arnold focused his energies and talents into the development of the BUT lines. The results were to speak for themselves.

In 1973 the company received just rewards for its efforts when it won the Queens Award for Export Achievement.

The late 70s saw the introduction of a new range of turkeys to replace the Triple 5 and Triple 6. These were: the Big 5; BUT 8; BUT 9; and the Big 6, all of which showed considerable performance advantages over their previous counterparts and indeed, over other competitive products. These began to accelerate BUT's increase in market share but sadly, the death of Rupert Chalmers Watson meant that he was never to witness the high flying achievement of his company in later years. At the

close of this decade BUT continued to thrive. In 1978, BUT was approached by Hubbard Farms, a subsidiary of the pharmaceutical company, Merck and Co. Inc., with a view to acquisition. This was finalised on December 11th.

The 1980s opened with BUT establishing its own company in the USA, called British United Turkeys of America. This new subsidiary was built with the capacity to supply around 40 per cent of the North American market which accounted for nearly 60 per cent of the world market at the time! This was a successful move for the company and by 1987, the year that the company celebrated its 25th anniversary with a luncheon at Warren Hall, BUT

Above: *A tier brooder for day old to 3.5 week old poults.* **Below:** *Some of the early team.* **Bottom:** *The BUT Franchise Breeders Conference in 1977.*

was achieving considerable success. This year also saw the completion of BUT's second Research and Development farm in Cheshire.

In the years between 1990 and 1997 BUT sales increased by 22 per cent for parent stock hens against a background of increased productivity by breeder and commercial activities. Since 1992, £11 million has been invested in a building and refurbishment programme for the company's breeding farms, including the Oaktree Farm near Chester. The 1990s were also a decade of growth for the company and new growth areas were established in Eastern Europe, the former Soviet Union and Asia. More turkey was consumed by the established markets of Western Europe, Israel and North America. Indeed, such is the stock's popularity in countries such as the UK, USA, Canada, France, Ireland, Italy, Holland, Germany, Hungary, Poland, Spain and Portugal that, by the end of the 1990s, BUT became the world's leading market supplier in turkeys.

BUT now has production agreements for Grandparents in France, Israel, Northern Ireland, America and New Zealand and the Sister Company BUTA has flourished.

Despite the worldwide nature of the business, BUT has maintained strong links with its Cheshire roots and is well known throughout the local farming community.

The most senior management in the company have put in over 200 years service between them, averaging over 25 years each, and over 40 per cent of the staff have put in more than 20 years service for the breeding company. The staff turnover is only 6 per cent! These figures show the loyalty of BUT's staff. With this level of commitment, combined with the innovative approach of the company, there is no doubt that British United Turkeys Limited will continue to play a major role in the world turkey industry in the future.

Above: *The free range turkeys at the Chester premises.*
Right: *The premises today.*

Chester Library

Both pictures: Although taken from slightly different angles, these two photographs show the progress of the Newgate Street and Grosvenor-Laing development during 1964, which was to result in the Grosvenor Precinct shopping centre. The first photograph *(above),* taken in May 1964, shows that rather depressing first phase when much is being knocked down and nothing discernible has taken shape. Men are burrowing away in the ground like moles, and judging from the state of the roofs, the buildings to the right of the Ambassadors Restaurant are next on the list for demolition. The 1960s was, of course, a decade of radical redevelopment and huge changes. Modernisation and tradition stand side-by-side in this picture, with the imposing presence of Chester Cathedral seemingly brooding over the transformation taking place beneath it. Not that the Cathedral had been immune to change, having evolved through church to abbey, and finally to Cathedral, over the course of its 1000 year history. Also Newgate Street itself was once known as Fleshmongers' Lane, an echo of Medieval times when streets were named after the goods produced or sold there.

Six months on *(left),* in November 1964, the Grosvenor-Laing development was definitely taking more shape. The centre of the photograph shows yet another delivery of Ready-Mix, and the outlines of a multi-storey building are beginning to emerge. Large-scale rebuilding in a city centre always causes unease in some quarters, and the publicity of the day was anxious to allay any fears. Within 12 months, it was argued, 'the grimness of the scaffolding and concrete' would be replaced by an ultra-modern covered shopping plaza, with red-brown brickwork to harmonise with the sandstone of the city walls and Newgate Street. Car-parking would be provided for 400 vehicles, and in the interior shoppers would enjoy controlled temperatures. The £3,000,000 Grosvenor-Laing scheme was to incorporate St Michael's Arcade. Shopping precincts were nothing new, for St Michael's Arcade had been built as early as 1910. Interestingly, its original white tile frontage had caused such a public outcry that the owner, the Duke of Westminster, had been forced to rebuild it in 'black and white' style. Shopping plazas are not to everyone's liking, and some still yearn for the more friendly and personal touch provided by local small shops. It may not be long, however, before the rise of Internet shopping makes us give a nostalgic sigh for the 'good old shopping precinct'!

Moving with the times

When Reg Lowe opened his furniture shop in Foregate Street in the early 1930s, he had no way of knowing that by the end of the century the modest business he founded would have developed into what is generally acknowledged to be Chester's premier removal company.

Back in those early days, household removals were merely a sideline, only undertaken when the firm's two vans were not being used to deliver new furniture. The two sides of the business continued until the early 1950s, but as the removals enterprise had by that time outstripped the retail, the shop was sold on to Cantors.

The removal company continued to grow, and in the late 1950s it was purchased by Paul Sweeney. Expansion was complicated at the time because of the difficulties in obtaining operators licences - a hurdle Mr Sweeney overcame by firstly taking over Fosters of Whipcord Lane and then F G Wright & Co (whose owner, interestingly, had at one time been Mayor of Chester). The purchase of the removals division of Brown's department store followed, allowing the company further expansion; another wise investment was container storage, and Lowes were one of the first in the country to recognise its potential. In 1961 Paul Sweeney was joined in the business by his son Gerald.

With the concentration on removals came experience - and with it, the gaining of the particular kind of expertise which led the company away from the old traditional ways of wrapping china and other breakables in straw

and old newspapers before packing in large tea chests and towards more modern packaging materials as they were developed. Today, the packaging used by Lowes of Chester include seven different types of carton, each of which has been especially designed to suit goods as diverse as books, clothing, linen and china. The old 'straw and newspapers' method has given way to bubble wrap, acid free tissue, flow pack, van wrap, sofa covers and special materials developed for goods being exported.

As the company developed, office and commercial relocations became a major part of Lowes' operations, each move being specifically tailored to the customer's requirements. Today's sophisticated office equipment -

Below: The opening of the new warehouse in 1968.
Bottom: One of the firm's earliest removal vehicles.

computers, printers, photocopiers, laboratory equipment and a huge variety of other complex machinery - demands a high degree of skill and advanced methods of packaging and handling when it comes to removing to new premises. The company can be justifiably proud of having found an innovative solution to every relocation problem they have encountered. When it comes to the practicalities of negotiating landings, corners, staircases and lifts they can offer their clients the very latest in specialised equipment, with power crawlers and barrows, lifting cages, fork lifts, powered hoists, mobile cranes and pallet trucks to deal with every item, be it large or small, awkwardly-shaped or extremely fragile. And when the relocation is completed and everything has been unpacked, Lowes do not regard the job as complete until they have walked around the building with their client to make sure that they are totally satisfied with the move.

It is this attention to detail that has helped to build up a list of many satisfied customers - among them county councils, chemical companies, investment bankers, major auction houses - who return to Lowes time and again with their every expansion and relocation.

Lowes - today part of the Whittle Group of companies - regards the training and expertise of their long-serving staff as the key to their technical superiority - and a great deal hangs on their professional know-how. At the beginning of every move, a consultation with the client will establish exactly what will be needed in the way of equipment and packing crates for the often vast amount of documents and paperwork collected by every company.

Above: A Lowe's van in the centre of Chester in the 1970s.
Right: Two vans in the 1980s.

When a company decides to relocate, the move often involves the relocation of a number of members of staff to different parts of the country or even overseas, and the Whittle Group have not neglected this vital aspect of customer care. The Group's experience in the field of international removals stretches back over a hundred years, and their experts are familiar with documentation requirements and the intricacies of British and foreign law. Their enviable track record led to official recognition from the British Standards Institute and membership of the British Association of Removers, both of whom demand a high standard of customer care and quality of service from their members.

From humble beginnings in a yard at the back of Queens Street to a purpose-built container facility at Sealand Road has taken Lowes of Chester on a long and fascinating journey, not only in the many hundred of miles they have travelled along the way, but in the gaining of the kind of professionalism that leaves nothing to chance.

Designing for the future

There is a saying that 'constant change is here to stay', and the Biggins Sargent partnership of architects and consultants have found more truth than most in the old adage. From modest beginnings in an office in Eastgate Row North almost half a century ago, the practice has grown into a large and well-respected firm based in the beautifully-restored 19th century Mold wing of Chester railway station.

It was 1952 when Ronald Biggins founded the practice, and the variety of work taken on quickly resulted in their gaining a reputation for excellence in the city. Their first major project was producing the design for a 700-ft long fibre-board manufacturing mill in Queensferry. The mill was completed in 1956 - the year which saw Britain and Egypt in a nose-to-nose conflict over Suez. The conflict abroad had a knock-on effect at home, but after an initial setback the fortunes of the partnership took a sharp upward turn.

The Festival of Britain in 1951 was largely responsible for new concepts in building design, and as post-war building schemes began to take off, a tremendous flood of work flowed into the office in Eastgate Row North. Space was suddenly at a premium, and a move to larger premises in in Boughton was necessary. An immense variety of different projects followed in places as far apart as the Scilly Isles, Northern Ireland, and the Shetland Islands in the UK, and in several overseas locations in Holland, France, and even further afield.

The growing influence and reputation of the practice led to the establishing of branch offices in Gloucester, Wolverhampton, London and Bristol. As the number of branches grew, so, of course, did the number of partners, associates and staff - and the Biggins Sargent Partnership became a recognised and respected name around the country.

In Chester and the surrounding area, a growing number of important buildings were designed by the partnership. Schools, colleges, public buildings of all sorts, health and hostel buildings, industrial and commercial projects, bank work and housing developments were completed. The Biggins Sargent Partnership were also responsible for the design of the ambitious £1.6 million expansion scheme embarked upon by the prestigious King's School in Chester.

A particularly exciting development came about during the 1970s, when Biggins Sargent became involved in the exploration for North Sea Oil. Eventually the partnership found itself moving more and more towards a particular expertise in conservation work. And thereby hangs a tale....

Above left: *John Sargent (left) and Ron Biggins, co-founders of the firm.* ***Below:*** *The redevelopment of the corner of Eastgate Street/Northgate Street at The Cross. This was the first major alteration to the Rows in the twentieth century.*

Despite being known as one of Chester's finest Victorian buildings, the Mold Wing of Chester railway station had lain derelict since it was destroyed by fire in the late 1960s. Exposed to the whims of British weather, the building had suffered badly both inside and out. Nevertheless, the Grade II Star listed building, designed by Francis Thompson back in 1847, was acquired by the partnership in 1980 for use as their new headquarters. The restoration project presented a huge challenge which was destined to cost more than £100,000, part of which was funded by various Listed Building grants. Six architects from the partnership were involved in the renovation, and the magnificently restored building was officially declared open by the Duke of Westminster.

The 4,000 square feet of largely open-plan offices made a fitting background for the drastic changes which were

by then taking place in design methods. Architectural drawings have traditionally been the product of drawing board, T-squares, pens and pencils. But by the 1980s the gigantic computers of the 1950s had shrunk with the advances in technology, and exciting new software was being designed. By the 1990s sophisticated computer aided design programmes had taken over, and architects could effectively hang up their T-squares.

Toasted by his colleagues in brandy, whose 28-year vintage reflected his 28 years of service, founder Ronald Biggins retired in 1980. Along with other founding partners who have since retired, Mr Biggins still features as a consultant to the partnership.

Over the years, the present six partners - David Patchitt (managing), Tony Reddy, Garry Bubb, Simon Johnson, Neil Robson and Terry Roberts - had emerged from former employees, and were therefore in a position to carry forward the character of the firm as a truly Cestrian entity. Their commitment has from the beginning been to provide well-designed, well-constructed buildings on cost and on budget, which will fulfil all the operator's requirements.

Their plans for the continuity of the practice continue well into the new millennium, helping to meet the ever changing demands of our built environment.

Above left: *The insertion of the new Crown Court into the courtyard of Chester Castle.* ***Top:*** *The restoration of the Mold Wing of Chester Station as the practice offices of the company between 1980 and 1989.*

A city marketed to attract the shopper

The history of Chester Market is a long and distinguished one, filled with chapters of continual progress and success. The city of Chester itself, like most old towns, is of ancient institution. As one of the old time market towns, Chester, never to be left behind, has always kept up to pace with developments in market trading. So, as all over the world there have been markets and fairs for the periodical gathering together of goods for sale, Chester has always managed to match these trends and facilitate them with the existence of a market.

In fact, the city of Chester has benefited from the existence of a market from as far back as early Roman times. The market was established due to a significant demand from traders who wanted to conduct their business in the city. The traders found Chester attractive because of the presence of soldiers in the town with lots of money to spend and the fruitful promise of lots of sold goods!

The lively city of Chester, with its vibrant history and heritage, has actually been attracting discerning shoppers and those with an eye for a bargain for nearly a thousand years! Although the very earliest mention of the existence of a market in Chester was in the year 1139, it was not until many years later that a shopping charter was first issued. The city's first shopping charter was, in fact, officially issued in the year 1208. It stated that, 'the men of Chester and their heirs' were granted the privilege of sole selling rights. These rights extended to everything except the annual fairs which

Below and right: Early views of stalls within the market.

were, in contrast, fair game for allcomers. These rights were confirmed in the year 1239 by Henry III, and the privilege of sole selling rights maintained its status in an unchanged form right up until the year 1506. It was in this year that the Great Charter was passed which also granted Chester its first Mayor.

The local people of the city wasted no time in making the most of the various shopping opportunities that had arisen. With their sharp eye for business, the people of Chester not only took advantage of the opportunities they were presented with but, did in fact, expand these opportunities to include, amongst many other enterprises, coal and cattle markets. Chester's rows and rows of traders built up a splendid reputation that stretched to places far and wide. Indeed, the now famous Rows were originally named after these lines of traders. The Rows themselves were various

and consisted of many different types of traders. Amongst them there was a Shoemakers Row, a Cooks Row and an Ironmongers Row. There was also a Pepper Alley and a Fish Shambles. These different areas of trade were closely followed by the Linen Hall and the Fruit, Root and Herb

The Chester market used to be situated on Northgate Street where it was located next to the Town Hall. From this location, the Market Hall, which traded for over 100 years, was opened on the 10th of March, 1863. This date was particularly poignant as it was also the Prince of Wales' wedding day! The market successfully traded from this location for many years until, in the year 1967, it was relocated to its current site in Princess Street. In 1997 the Princess Street Chester Market was able to celebrate its Pearl anniversary.

Today, Chester Market is run by Chester City Council. From Princess Street, the market opens six days a week, from Monday to Saturday. It contains up to 100 stalls offering a wide choice of the finest quality produce from foodstuffs to flowers, cosmetics and millinery! Indeed, as in ancient times gone by, Chester Market continues to attract the discerning shopper and hopes to continue to do so for many years to come.

Market. Most needs were catered for by the market. Whatever the shopper could possibly need, they could always find somewhere, in and amongst the multitude of stalls in the Rows of the market!

The shopping opportunities and trade of the Chester area continued to flourish and soon, horse, cloth and cheese fairs could also be found in the city. These fairs of old eventually became the forerunners of the magnificent array of shops that can be found in the city today. The bustling town centre market has always played a major part in the city's shopping life. The market itself, has been in existence and in operation for centuries, literally by order of King and qQueen!

Above and top: *1960s views of stalls within the market.*
Right: *The exterior of the market in the 1960s.*

Compassionate service from a local, independent family business

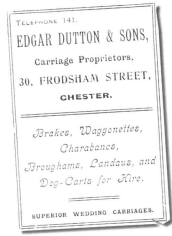

Dutton and Hallmark are one of the only independent, locally owned, family run Funeral Directors in the Chester area. The company has an interesting history which tells the tale of two separate and indeed very competitive firms, resolving their differences to become united once again, in business and in friendship!

The Dutton family have been involved in the business of funerals for as far back as the present members of the family can establish. The exact details of the family's history in the Funeral Directing business are not known. However, it is known that Thomas Dutton was working as a coffin maker as long ago as 1704! It was in fact, his great grandson, Edgar Dutton, that founded Edgar Dutton and Sons in the 1850s.

Edgar's father, Caleb Dutton, owned a Funeral Directors business in Forgate Street in Chester and had been running it from about 1800. Edgar had, in his youth, helped his father out by working for him in the business. Indeed, this experience proved to be invaluable later in Edgar's life when he summoned all his accumulated experience and knowledge of the industry and used it to set up his own business. Edgar established his new and burgeoning business at Lower Bridge Street in the 1850s and began trading as a Funeral

Directors and Carriage Proprietors under the name, Edgar Dutton and Sons.

With the help of his sons, John James and George Henry, Edgar's business soon began to flourish and was ever gaining a fine reputation with the people of the town of Chester and beyond. Edgar Dutton and Sons' trade, as makers of coffins and suppliers of hearses and carriages, also won it a high reputation with other Funeral Directors and Wheelwrights with which it conducted business. By the 1860s Edgar had become successful enough to be able to move his business to new and improved premises located at 9 Frodsham Street, Chester.

Left: An early business card. Below: Willy Hallmark in the 1920s outside Overleigh Cemetery. Bottom: Edgar Dutton with his back to the camera, Harry holding the horse and John James in the doorway.

It was at these new premises that Edgar Dutton first met and became friendly with the Hallmark family. The Hallmark family owned a catering business, W H Hallmark and Sons. Edgar established a friendship with the family and soon, he was able to start passing business their way. Indeed, the two families started to work in conjunction with each other and Edgar used their services to cater for funeral parties.

The two businesses both continued to thrive. In 1860, Edgar Dutton and Sons were able to move again, this time to 30 Frodsham Street, where they stayed for over 100 years. Unfortunately, in 1890 the Hallmark's decided to set up in business as a Funeral Directors. This meant that the two families were in direct competition with each other and as a consequence, they became sworn enemies and did not speak for the next 30 years!

In 1902, Edgar Dutton was made the Sheriff of Chester. This event was followed by a first for his business, in 1910, when it started to provide motorised funerals! During the first and second world wars, the business managed to organise many RAF and Army funerals, despite the absence of many young members of staff who were away serving their country in the war. In the 1930s Edgar's grandsons, Edgar junior and Thomas, took over the running of the

business and in 1936, Edgar Dutton and Sons became the last Funeral Directors to provide horse drawn funerals. W H Hallmark and Sons, on the other hand, experienced difficulties during these years and went into receivership, twice! The business was bought by the Griffin family in the 1940s and they ran it successfully until 1974.

It was in 1974 that W H Hallmark and Sons, and Edgar Dutton and Sons both closed their businesses due to ill health and problems with the premises. During the following years, Edgar's great grandson, Stephen Dutton, met and married Mr Griffins' daughter, Eurwen. This union led to the reunion and re-establishment of the two original businesses, as the couple decided to set up a Funeral Directors business under the name, Dutton and Hallmark. The business soon resumed its former success. In 1997, it added another first to its history by re-introducing horse drawn funerals. However, the business owns the largest funeral fleet in the area and so can provide the use of limousines if preferred. Today, Stephen and Eurwen take pride in their company's history and aim to follow in Edgar Dutton's tradition of providing a friendly, personal and compassionate service to the people of Chester.

Above left: *Edgar Dutton & son's team during the second world war.* ***Top:*** *Edgar Dutton conducting a funeral in Chester about 1912.* ***Below:*** *The company's new Armstrong-Siddeley fleet in 1958.*

Tailoring progress within the constraints of traditionalism

The Menswear Specialists, Cochrane's of Chester, located in Bridge Street Row has an interesting history dating as far back as 1906. It was in this year that William Cochrane opened his first Gentleman's Outfitters shop in the town at Chester Cross.

Before founding their business in Chester, it is thought that William and his wife had owned several shops in Liverpool, Southport, and the Miller Arcade in Preston. However, the couple decided to sell these shops and as a step towards semi-retirement moved to Chester. There, they opened a shop at the Cross initially called, The Belfast Shirt and Collar Company, but later renamed as, Ye Olde Tan Glove Shoppe. The shop specialised in socks, gloves and regimental ties. The Cochrane's impressive range of goods proved to be extremely popular and the business began to thrive. Indeed, amongst one of the shop's distinguished customers was the Duchess of Westminster who frequently purchased ladies gloves from the Cochrane's.

It was not long before the first shop became successful enough to enable Mrs Cochrane to open another shop, this time specialising in ladieswear. The new shop was opened at 39 Bridge Street Row under the name, Camilla. Mrs Cochrane started to introduce menswear to the shop and eventually, it became wholly devoted to this range. As a result, some time around the year 1920, a new branch of Camilla was opened at 37 Bridge Street Row trading in ladieswear and as a milliners. However, the shop was to enjoy only a brief spell as a ladieswear specialist as, when Mrs Cochrane retired in about 1926, her husband continued the lease but changed the contents to menswear.

Two of the Cochrane's four sons worked in the family business. William was put in charge of the Cross shop and Bruce was put in charge of the shop at 37 Bridge Street Row. Interestingly enough, the family managed to fully establish themselves during a notoriously difficult

Left: *William Cochrane, founder of the company.*
Below and bottom: *Early window displays.*

now it would cost over £200. In 1949 a suit cost £8.15.8 compared to about £300 in the shop today!

The 1980s brought with them several developments for the company. It was during this decade that, with the onset of more foreign holidays, leisure wear started to become popular. With the help of the Managing Director, Mr Hancock, Cochrane's managed to change with the times without abandoning traditionalism or alienating their long standing customers. Indeed, the shop's stock became gradually more and more colourful as did the window displays, which were now made into a sales feature.

With some regret, in 1987, due to hefty rates and rent increases, the shop at Chester Cross had to be closed. The advantage of this event however, was that the company could now concentrate all its efforts on the success of the shop in Bridge Street Row. On Mr Hancock's retirement in 1988, Mr Seed became Managing Director of Cochrane's and continued to maintain the company's thriving success. In 1990, the shop front was painted green and gold and in 1999, the shop underwent further changes when it was refurbished to achieve an up-to-date but traditional look.

Under Michael Hall, who became managing director in 1998, progress will continue, always within the constraints of traditionalism, Cochrane's of Chester will no doubt continue to provide an expert and specialist service to the people of the town for many years to come.

This page: *The interior in the 1960s.*

economic time. They survived the first world war, the General Strike and the 1930s depression. The business became a Limited company in 1935 and during the second world war, the only disruption was the absence of one of its employees, Mr Just, who had gone away to war, but returned in 1944. He subsequently became managing director until the mid 1980s.

The Cochrane's business continued to go from strength to strength and the shops gained a high reputation in the town. The brown shop front, with its green tiles, became a permanent fixture in the Victorian Arcade. In 1964, the shop underwent a refit, the old glass and mahogany counters were replaced with modern fixtures and the lighting was improved. It was not until 1970 however, that the old procedure of writing receipts on dockets was replaced with the use of a modern cash register. The shop stocked several well known brands at the time including, Double Two and Viyella. The shirts were all cotton, had detachable collars, and had to be in white, blue or cream! The prices of the stock also differed in comparison with today's prices. In 1953 a raincoat cost, £7.10.0, whilst

Binding experience with expertise to form a volume of success

T he history of the booksellers, Bookland and Company Limited is an interesting one, dating back to the year 1935 and establishing subsequent close links to the city of Chester.

It was in this year that Henry James Elsley made the ambitious decision to give up his job as a solicitor and with the help of his wife, Ethel, set up his own business. The couple chose book selling as their new venture, not because of Henry James' literary name, but because they saw a gap in the market. Despite the fact that the country was in the depths of depression and suffering severe unemployment, there was a feeling that education was improving and as a result, books and reading were becoming increasingly popular. It was in this climate that the Elsleys opened their first shop in Liverpool in 1935 under the name, Bookland.

It was not long before the burgeoning business began to flourish. This initial success meant that the Elsleys were able to expand their business and open a second Bookland shop. Chester was chosen as the location for the new shop and premises at 19 Bridge Street were purchased. These premises had a cobbled floor and were generally in a state of dilapidation. Consequently, the shop had to be completely renovated before it was opened. Once it did open, the shop was extremely successful. Indeed, its popularity was further increased when Henry's entrepreneurial spirit led him to spot another gap in the market and take the unusual step of opening a lending library within the shop.

Just before the advent of the second world war, the Elsleys opened another book shop in Chester. The old Odeon building had become vacant and was chosen as the location of the second Chester Bookland. Ethel Elsley combined bringing up the Elsley family with doing the accounts, buying the stationery and dealing with staff matters in the new shop. However, after the cessation of the war, in the year 1945, Ethel was joined and assisted in her work by her son, John Brian Elsley. John had completed an apprenticeship with another bookseller and consequently, joined his family's business already complete with relevant experience and expertise.

Below: *A print of the Ancient Crypt.*
Bottom: *The premises circa 1905.*

The post war hunger for learning increased the demand for the library and for school supply work. As a result, Henry Elsley made frequent trips to London to search out more stock in order to meet this need. It was in the year 1951 that another of the Elsley's children, Olive, joined the family business. Indeed, Olive and her brother John opened another Bookland shop in Stafford in this year. It was also during these formative years of Bookland's history that other branches were opened in Wallasey, Colwyn Bay, Ellesmere Port and Wolverhampton.

The 1960s opened with a sad event for the Elsley family with the death of Ethel Elsley. It was also during this time that the shop at 19 Bridge Street was closed. New premises at 12 Bridge Street were bought to compensate for this closure but unfortunately, because the premises were leased to tenants, they could not be utilised until 1978. However, in 1966 another shop was able to be opened in Chester at 7 Newgate Row and further branches were also opened in Bangor and Newcastle between 1966 and 1967. The decade ended successfully for the Elsleys as in 1968, the business became a Limited Company.

Sadly, in 1977 Henry James Elsley died. However, Henry's son John took over the running of the Company that his father had founded over 40 years previously. The first major event for Bookland and Company Limited under John's leadership, was the opening of 12 Bridge Street in 1978. This unique shop, situated in one of Chester's best specimens of black and white architecture, houses probably the second oldest crypt in the city dating from as far back as 1270-80! During the following two decades the Company continued to

thrive and further branches of Bookland were able to be opened. In 1981, a shop was opened in Wrexham followed by the opening of another shop in Blackburn in 1986, one in Warrington in 1988, and another at Chester College in 1993. The year 1994 marked the opening of a new chapter for the Company. It was in this year that the founder's grandson, Richard James, became Managing Director of Bookland and Company Limited. This appointment was followed by the opening of the Company's 16th branch in Nantwich in 1997. Today, Bookland and Company Limited employs a total of 128 people who all play their part in ensuring that the Elsley family business is ready to turn yet another page in its long history of success.

Above left and top: *The interior.*
Below: *The premises today.*

From quill pen to computer keyboard

Few firms can make the claim today that they are still practising under their original name. Not so Henry R Davis & Co, however. Their history goes back a long way, and today's members of staff are justifiably proud of their achievements. Not only have they retained the name of the founder, but the firm is still banking with NatWest, who were of course the National Provincial Bank when Henry Davis put up his brass plate outside his offices in Cathedral Chambers and took up his quill pen back in 1912. Interestingly, an old advertisement card picturing the lovely old building reveals that until at least 1910 this was the Doric Hotel. Henry R Davis & Co have remained at their original premises for an incredible 88 years.

Those years just before, and during, the first world war, were difficult ones for any fledgling business, and setting up as a Certified Accountant and Chartered Secretary was no different. Henry Davis set up small branch offices in Holywell, Shotton and Northwich where he spent a day or so every week - which meant of course that many miles of road had to be covered. There was no stylish new motor car for the young Henry Davis, however - not even one of the economical Model T Fords, brought out by Henry Ford

four years earlier. A motor bike and sidecar were the transport used by Henry as he bowled along the Cheshire roads accompanied by his secretary and personal assistant Miss Swindley, who had joined the firm in 1914 just as 'the war to end all wars' began.

As the firm expanded, so did the workforce. George Hargreaves joined Henry Davis in 1934 - the first, it turned out, of three members of the Hargreaves family

Above left: The firm's Hunter Street premises.
Below: From left to right: Tony Travers, Harold Shaw, Roger Hargreaves, George Hargreaves, David Atkinson and Brian Stonehouse. Bottom: This picture dates from 1987 and shows 24 past chairmen of the Chester and North Wales branch of the Liverpool Institute of Chartered Accountants receiving their Chairman's medal from their immediate predecessor.

who were to become 'part of the furniture' - George's son Roger entered the firm in 1964 (and still remains there today), followed in turn by his own son James in the last year of the 20th century.

It was almost by accident that George Hargreaves joined the firm. As a newly qualified Chartered Accountant he first of all looked for work in his native Bolton. The dark days of the Depression still overshadowed the 1930s, however, and for the huge number of people out of work the prospects of employment were slim. A national Unemployment Fund had been created in 1928 - the 'dole' of a pitiful sum that was barely enough to keep alive on - yet many saw it as encouraging laziness, and the meagre unemployment benefits were actually cut by ten per cent in 1931. It was an anxious time for the young man looking for work in his chosen field. Not a few were forced by circumstances into taking any employment they could find, including a fellow-student of George Hargreaves, who qualified at the same time - yet found himself joining the police force!

On finding that no suitable positions were vacant in Bolton, George began to look further afield. Thankfully he came to rest in Chester, in the offices of Henry R Davis & Co. An interesting observation is his starting pay of £4.10s per week, which was typical for a newly qualified Chartered Accountant in the 1930s; inflation has reduced the size of this pay packet today to the price of a single CD! The pound in your pocket certainly went much further back then, as we can see from a number of interesting receipts which survive from the period; sums such as £5.2s or £16.7.6d were typical fees charged for work carried out for clients at the time. George Hargreaves was to become Chairman of the Chester and North Wales branch of the Liverpool Society of Chartered Accountants

in 1961, as indeed were his partners, Harold Shaw, in 1969 and Roger Hargreaves in 1980.

The major expansion of the practice took place in the 1960s when Harold Shaw joined the partnership and the firm converted from certified to chartered accountants. A whole new range of clients in the engineering and manufacturing fields were added to the existing farming, retail and professional base. There followed a considerable increase in staff and partners as evidenced by the accompanying photographs. Long service awards are par for the course amongst the loyal staff and partners at Henry R Davis & Co and many of the present incumbents have between 25 and 42 years of service to their names and are still going strong!

From their very earliest days, Henry R Davis & Co made it their aim to offer each individual client a speedy and cost conscious service, relying heavily on the value of personal contact and an air of permanence and reliability in the community. This did not mean, however, that the firm stood still. As modern technology changed and advanced, so did their methods of work. The foresighted attitude led to Henry R Davis being the first among local accountants to install computers for the preparation of clients' annual accounts.

Down the years the firm's name has become synonymous with excellence of customer care, and as they move into the 21st century, the high principles first established by Henry Davis himself will remain as Henry R Davis & Co continues to maintain their excellent service to the business community.

Top: *Partners and staff at a retirement party for Ted Andrews in 1987.*

A busy shopping day on Eastgate Street, captured in August 1951.

Acknowledgments

Robert L. Astrella

Chester Archives

Chester Library, Libraries & Archives, Cheshire County Council

Thanks are also due to
Peter Thomas who penned the editorial text
and Ann Ramsdale for her copywriting skills